Why Does My Dog Do That?

Why Does My Dog Do That?

Comprehensive answers to the
50+ questions that every dog owner asks

Ivy Press

First published in 2008 by
Ivy Press
210 High Street, Lewes,
East Sussex BN7 2NS, U.K.
www.ivypress.co.uk

British Library Cataloguing-in-Publication Data
A catalogue record for this book is available from the British Library

ISBN: 978-1-905695-75-1

Printed in China
10 9 8 7 6 5

Ivy Press
This book was conceived, designed, and produced by iBall, an imprint of Ivy Press.

Creative Director Peter Bridgewater
Publisher Jason Hook
Editorial Director Caroline Earle
Art Director Clare Harris
Senior Editor Lorraine Turner
Design J.C. Lanaway
Concept Clare Barber
Illustrator Michael Chester
Consultant Veterinarian Dr. Shawn Messonnier

The questions and answers in this book relate to individual cases and should not be used as a substitute for a veterinarian's advice. Please see your veterinarian if you have any concerns about your dog or its behavior.

Contents

Introduction

If you live with a dog, you will already have some idea of how well dogs in general have adapted to the human way of life. Your pet keenly accompanies you to all the activities in your life that interest him—and likely sleeps through all the ones that don't. What you may be less aware of is the canine way of life that your dog has adapted from. Many of the behaviors that raise the question "Why does he DO that?" arise from your dog's hardwiring—the deep-down patterns that make him a dog, not a person. It's these questions that this book sets out to answer.

Most of the flexibility in the human/canine relationship comes from the dog. Dogs are remarkably flexible, and cope well with many things that they cannot relate to in their own world. They have a good idea of which parts of human behavior they need to understand, and which they can just let roll past. Humans are not nearly so adaptable—whereas it's plain to see that dogs often write off the manners of their owners as simply "how they are," humans tend to offer up interpretations for uncompromising canine behavior. This can give rise to some comical misunderstandings; however, sometimes the results are more serious, and a dog that has simply

been communicating in a way that comes naturally will be categorized as irritable, unpredictable, or worse still, aggressive.

So it's not only interesting to know why he really does do the things that have always puzzled you—it's important, too. Some of the questions we've included are those that every dog owner will recognize: Why does my dog turn around before he lies down? Why does he move away when I try to hug him? Why does he always have to sniff the wrong end of an approaching dog? Others may be more unusual, but you will have seen dogs behaving in all the ways we discuss. And if you pride yourself on always treating your dog as a dog, not a surrogate human, some of the answers may surprise you. They will also help to turn the tables and encourage you to ask yourself why *you* behave in a certain way. After all, your dog behaves like a canid, while you are a homonid, a sophisticated great ape—and a lot of your behavior (working with your hands, and endless communication, especially by facial expression) is just, well, what apes do.

Read on to understand why your dog *does* do that, and to understand more about the human/canine relationship. All you'll need then is to find a means of explaining to your dog why *you* behave the way that you do.

Chapter one

From puppy to adult

Growing puppies learn an astounding amount in a very short time: at birth they can't hear or see; by two weeks their eyes are open and they're beginning to explore; and from then on **it's a rapid trajectory with many milestones, all the way to adulthood at between one and two years.** Dogs mature at different ages, and some of the larger breeds are slower to become full-fledged adults. The key period, from most dog owners' point of view, is the time between which a puppy leaves its mother and joins its new human "family," usually at around eight weeks, through to adolescence. The first month away from its family, at between eight and 12 weeks, is key for ensuring that the puppy has as many positive new experiences as possible. This is the time during which his socialization skills form, and a wide range of enjoyable possibilities on his "what to expect" radar will help him understand that the unfamiliar is part of normal life. Thereafter, puppyhood poses challenges to most owners, although most will find that the benefits far outweigh the problems.

Why does my puppy … scratch and yawn during training class?

Q At home, my puppy is cheerful, self-confident, and into everything. At her first couple of socialization and puppy-training classes, though, she spent a lot of time sitting down and scratching vigorously (she never scratches at home). When I encouraged her to join in with the group she kept yawning, too. Was she suddenly itchy? Or tired? Or was there some other problem?

SHE'S NOT REALLY SLEEPY but yawning sends a signal to other dogs that she isn't pushy or presumptuous about her rather daunting new surroundings.

A It's likely that you have a cautious puppy and she was feeling uncertain. Chances are that she didn't feel either itchy or tired, but stressed—yawning and sudden scratching bouts can send an "include me out" signal to other dogs. Among the experts, opinions differ as to whether dogs use this sort of behavior on purpose, to sign their lack of ease in a situation, or whether the behavior is instinctive and other dogs have learned to recognize the body language (much as humans might recognize that someone shifting constantly in their seat is uncomfortable, whether or not the subject is conscious of what he or she is doing). **Yawning or scratching are exclusive actions: they don't imply any invitation to another dog to join in or to investigate.**

Your puppy may overcome her nerves and learn to enjoy the classes—some puppies bounce through early training filled with eagerness, while others, particularly if they haven't had much experience of meeting several unfamiliar dogs together, seem to feel overwhelmed. If she still seems uncomfortable after two or three tries, think about gradually increasing her exposure to other dogs one or two at a time, in an open space where she has plenty of room. If you know anyone with calm, friendly adult dogs who aren't easily fazed—not every adult dog is tolerant of puppies, so ask around—a couple of gentle play dates would be a great way to build her confidence and help to make a roomful of dogs seem less intimidating.

SPECIES WATCH

Many animals and birds will behave in a way that resembles grooming when uncomfortable; in fact, in birdwatching, one sign that you're getting too close to a nesting bird is if it starts to clean itself exaggeratedly, preening and repeatedly wiping its bill. Most domestic cat owners are familiar with the cat mantra when it is feeling uncomfortable or under pressure: if in doubt, wash.

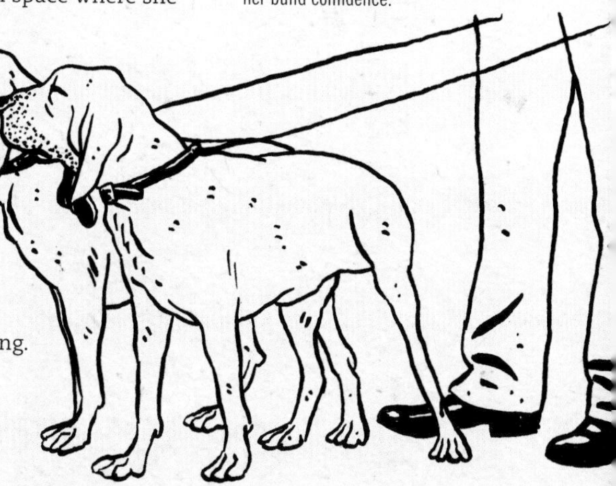

INTRODUCE YOUR PUPPY to calm, friendly dogs to help her build confidence.

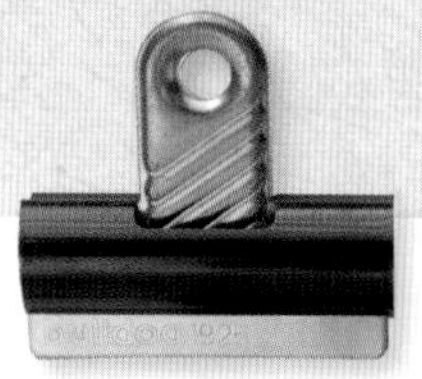

Why does my dog … keep correcting my puppy so firmly?

Q We have a five-year-old dog who is usually very mellow and relaxed. We recently got a three-month-old puppy (it wasn't a planned acquisition; we were asked to take on a rescue pup and felt that we had the time to commit to him) and, while the two seem to be getting along well enough, our older dog corrects the puppy very firmly when he gets too pushy. Sometimes the puppy squeaks and squeals and it sounds as though he's afraid. Yet the two cuddle up together and sleep in the evenings. Should we be worried? And why does our older dog feel he has to behave this way?

IT'S AN OLDER DOG'S JOB to quell presumption in a puppy and to introduce him to the social order of his new family.

A Unless your older dog is actually doing damage to your pup, you probably don't need to worry. Older dogs naturally correct puppies and teach them manners (often much more effectively than humans do) and, on the whole, seem to manage this without problems. Sometimes it can be comical to watch a puppy trying things out on his elder and getting a sharp rebuff in response. **Puppies can make quite a noisy fuss about a slight correction** but, if you watch your older dog closely, you're likely to find out that, even if he looks as though he's snapping, he's actually holding his jaws carefully open. As puppies get older, a senior dog may also give what behaviorists call a correction bite, which is a fast, economical bite that makes contact but is highly controlled and doesn't break the skin.

PUPPIES TEACH ONE ANOTHER tolerance in the rough-and-tumble play that's natural in a litter.

Dogs who don't live in human households have to establish order in their society, and puppies are effectively taught the skills they need to survive. At first, small puppies are disciplined only by their mothers and, when they are very young, such "discipline" may consist simply of the mother getting up and moving away when the pups want to feed.

As they get older, puppies start to be handled slightly more roughly by their mother, who may nip them if they get out of line, and other adult dogs may discipline them, too. Learning that he can't always get his own way will help to turn your puppy into a polite adult. If you honestly feel that, at times, the correction is getting too severe, don't separate the dogs because this will only teach your puppy that he doesn't have to sort problems on his own; instead, distract both dogs and play with them together or put them through a basic training exercise. This will refocus the pair of them and remind them that you're ultimately the one in charge.

SPECIES WATCH

Animals who live socially also teach their young the life skills they need to know. An adult dog may teach a pup good manners, but in a wild dog or wolf pack the cubs would also be helped with hunting techniques. Cats, from lions to tabbies, also impart hunting skills, while meerkats will train their young by bringing them prey (in the meerkat world this might often be a scorpion or a large beetle) to finish off.

Why does my puppy ... hate her crate?

Q When I brought my puppy home, I was advised by our vet to buy her a crate; he said that she would come to consider it as her den and that it would be a quiet place for her to feel safe, as well as a good way of ensuring she got used to sleeping in the kitchen quietly and happily. But my puppy seems to hate her crate—she avoids going in it at all costs, and if I try to encourage her in with treats, she'll hide in a corner and cower away to avoid being put in it forcibly. What should I do?

COZY DEN OR LONELY CAGE? How your puppy views her crate may depend a good deal on the way in which she's been introduced to it.

A First, has she ever been put in her crate against her will, or left there too long to keep her out of the way? Most puppies do learn to enjoy their crates as a refuge from the busy new world of their human home, but they need to be introduced to a crate carefully. Maybe she's been left shut in too long, and associates it with loneliness rather than security. Maybe she's been there after she's made a mess—dogs have a natural dislike of soiling where they sleep, so if she's had any long periods in her crate, that might be a factor, too.

MOST PUPPIES WILL ENJOY a comfortable playpen, even in the rare cases that they just can't get along with a crate.

Whatever the cause, it's her prerogative to express her feelings. Don't coerce her into her crate—it will make matters worse, because she might become afraid of you as well. **Try gently tempting her in with a treat or a favorite toy, but without closing the door—she may be happier to snack or play in there with the door open.** Make her crate cozy with a familiar blanket. Don't shut her in at all until she is going in of her own accord. If you get to a point at which she seems happy to go into her crate, give her a treat, then shut her in for just a minute, without making any fuss, before opening the door. If she feels that going into her crate is her decision, she's more likely to favor it.

A few dogs never learn to love their crates, and if yours is one of them, a child's playpen set up with a cozy basket may prove more palatable. Whichever you choose, never "park" your puppy on her own for a long time except at nighttime when she's ready for sleep; boredom can trigger problem behavior later on.

Why has my dog... suddenly turned so rebellious?

Q Our first dog has just hit the six-month stage. We were warned that doggy adolescence can be quite testing on owners, but we never realized how bad it could be—our much-loved, obedient, cuddly puppy seems to have suddenly become blind and deaf to all the training and practice that he used to love. He chews things he shouldn't, he barks, he roughhouses just when he's been told to calm down, and he constantly seems to be testing us. How can we get through this stage, and when can we expect it to end?

MOST DOGS GO THROUGH a contrary "teenage" phase, just like their human equivalents, but how extreme it is can vary a lot between individual dogs.

A If it's any comfort, you're not alone. The majority of dogs that are given up to shelters are handed over at seven or eight months old. Owners will have been warned about the hooligan stage, but faced with the appeal of an eight-week-old puppy not many take the information in, and this can lead to some real canine tragedies down the line. Two pieces of good news: first, most dogs are beginning to calm down at one year of age, and are responsible citizens at two, although larger breeds may take a little longer to mature.

Even better, **there are numerous ways you can head your puppy's abstraction and plain teenage rebellion off at the pass and work with him during this crucial time.** A strong bond formed with a canine adolescent is especially rewarding.

BOND WITH YOUR DOG while he's a teenager and you'll be strengthening your future relationship with him.

Patience and consistency will help. Plenty of energetic exercise; a nutritious, balanced diet; a calm voice; and a sense of humor will all be useful, too. Adolescence can hit different breeds at different ages, but by six months most dogs will be becoming more adventurous and exploratory. An unneutered male will be producing testosterone at an extremely high rate, and a female dog will be coming up to her first season; both sexes will probably have a growth spurt, and the arrival of adult teeth will mean a greater-than-ever need to chew. Add a hair-trigger response to arousal and it's clear why your dog will need plenty of loving understanding to get him through this stage. Keep reinforcement training to little and often, and make sure that your puppy has an energetic exercise session, an enjoyable play session, and at least ten minutes of training (the latter two can often be combined) every single day. If he's given plenty to do, there's much less chance of his getting into mischief.

SPECIES WATCH

While it may seem never-ending to wait for a slow-maturing puppy of a large breed to grow up, spare a thought for elephant parents; teenage elephants don't mature until they're 15 or 16 years of age. Gorillas are another species who take a while to mature (around 12 years), as are hippopotamuses (seven to nine years). And of course humans are notoriously slow-maturing, too.

Why does my dog... not take things away from my puppy?

Q Our new puppy has settled in quite well with our older dog, but the latter dog certainly rules the roost. I was watching them the other day, though, and I saw something I didn't understand: the puppy had a hold on a chew toy that they both enjoy, and the adult dog was watching her closely. He obviously wanted the toy and he could easily have taken it away from the pup by force, but he didn't; instead he watched rather wistfully for a minute or two, then sighed and lay down. Why didn't he just take the toy he wanted?

THEY BOTH WANT the same thing, but the older dog is abiding by the canine rule of possession. The puppy gets to keep what's already in her possession.

A Behaviorists have noticed the situation you describe in many adult dogs interacting with puppies, although opinions vary as to the reason for it. Dogs generally seem to follow a "finders-keepers" rule if the treasure is already in the possession of an individual. You don't mention what age your puppy is, but even quite young puppies, if they're firmly in charge of a desirable object, can often keep it, provided that they don't let their attention wander. It's possible, also, that your older dog is still exhibiting a degree of permissiveness toward your puppy; she's still young enough to avoid severe correction.

The well-respected writer and trainer Patricia McConnell defines "dominance" in the dog world as merely "a description of who gets the bone if two dogs want it, but [it doesn't] say anything about how the 'dominant' dog gets the bone." So even if your older dog rules the roost, it may be he doesn't think the chew toy is worth the conflict of taking it by force. As every owner knows, **dogs are great negotiators and most can accurately balance up the pros and cons of a canine situation in a heartbeat.**

The idea that social animals in the wild spend a lot of time fighting is a false one: fighting within one's own group is far too risky and tiring to indulge in when it's hard work simply surviving. So the arts of negotiation are hardwired into most dogs. If your puppy takes her eye off the chew toy for even a second, it's likely that your older dog will take it from her; if, however, she remains fully focused, it is hers to enjoy.

ONE BOWL EACH Even dinnertime can be surprisingly peaceful provided that everyone keeps their eyes on their own bowl.

Why does my puppy ... always push his luck with older dogs?

Q My six-month-old puppy is exuberant and enthusiastic about other dogs. He was introduced to a whole range of other dogs at the dog park as soon as he'd had his inoculations, and he seems to love them all. Problems sometimes arise, though, because he doesn't recognize when another dog may not want to play, and he will sometimes persist even when a dog is getting snappy and visibly irritated. We're often told that dogs are great communicators, so why doesn't he seem to realize when it's time to leave well alone?

IF A PUPPY IS PUSHY, an older dog may have to work his way through an escalating series of corrections before Junior finally gets the message.

A At six months, your puppy is on the brink of adolescence, and he isn't yet practiced at reading the signals. This doesn't mean that he won't learn tact in time (how often have you heard one owner tell another, after a snappy incident such as you describe, "Don't worry, he has to learn.")

Dogs are great communicators, but a large proportion of their communication is taught, mostly by other dogs.

Was your puppy the product of a single-pup litter? Canine behaviorists have noticed that single pups, without the constant low-level frustration of having to compete with siblings for milk and maternal attention, can turn into the sort of teenagers who don't have much capacity for understanding that they can't have what they want right now. Without any experience of frustration, they may try to insist.

IT REALLY *IS* JUST PLAY even though it may look a bit rough to human eyes; sometimes two "scrapping" dogs are simply enjoying themselves.

Even if he wasn't a lone kid, your pup clearly hasn't learned the rules of polite society yet. You're unlikely to have to sort out his gauche behavior by yourself—this is the sort of thing that other dogs are very good at. But don't neglect your responsibilities: if he is really bothering a dog that is getting seriously annoyed (or is looking stressed and worried), defuse the tension by getting your puppy to pay attention to you for a moment or two. Even if he is highly excited, it's usually possible to bring a six-month-old to your side with the judicious use of treats. If he's only being irritating, though, and the other dog's owners are relaxed about it, give him the chance to find out that his pushy behavior is more likely to earn him a nip on the nose than a satisfying game.

Why does my dog … remain so attached to her puppy blanket?

Q We got our puppy from a breeder and she came to us with a large square of blanket, described as something familiar from home to help her feel comfortable. Eight months later, she's nearly ten months old, and is well settled in to the household. She is invariably cheerful and seems happy, but she still cherishes her increasingly decrepit scrap of blanket and looks around for it regularly, particularly last thing in the evening when she's about to settle down for the night. It seems to me to have the same strong appeal for her as an ancient, well-loved teddy does for a child who is rapidly growing too old for it. My partner says this is a ridiculously anthropomorphic view. Which of us is right?

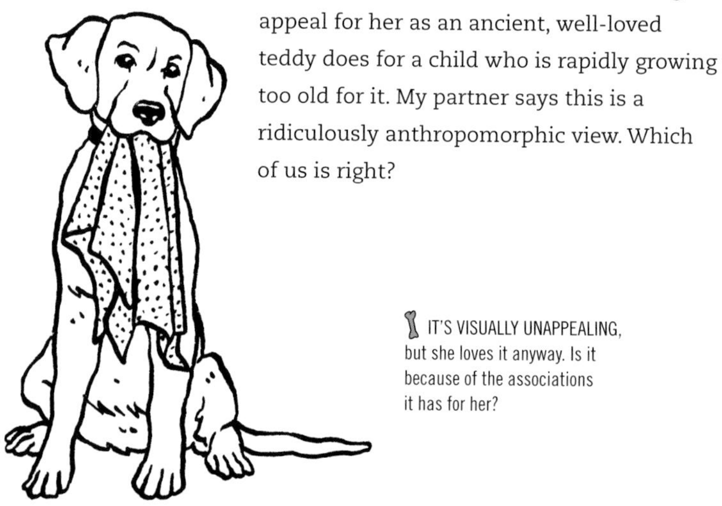

IT'S VISUALLY UNAPPEALING, but she loves it anyway. Is it because of the associations it has for her?

A This question takes us to the heart of the how-much-are-dogs-really-like-us debate. Does your puppy consciously like her blanket because it reminds her of her happy first weeks, cuddled up in a litter against the flank of her mother? Or is her affection for it something much less coherent than that, having more to do with its familiar smell and texture in her mouth? Whichever is the truth (and it may be between the two; also the well-chewed texture of the blanket probably appeals to her), the principal reason she loves it is likely to be its smell. **Most people are aware that dogs have a much stronger sense of smell than humans, but what they may not realize is just how much stronger it is: a dog's sense of smell is more than 44 times stronger than a human's.** It's hard to imagine the cacophony of smells that must assault their noses as they step outside. Your dog's blanket probably smells of security to her, and seems most important when she's going to bed.

HAPPY MEMORIES for a puppy are of being safe and warm with her siblings, which will be strongly identified by their smell.

A couple of years down the line, the grubby, tattered remnants of a once-respectable blanket may cause you to make faces, but it's best to leave your dog to decide when, or even whether, she wants to give up her treasure. Eventually it will disintegrate utterly and she'll forget about it. It's probably not coincidental that breeders have noted that it's those breeds who habitually like to mouth—usually retrieving breeds such as retrievers, spaniels, and labradors—who remain most devoted to these memorials to their puppyhood.

Why has my puppy … apparently forgotten his house training?

Q At six months old, our terrier puppy hadn't made a mess in the house for over a month. But the other night my partner shouted at him when she found a book he had chewed to pieces, and he rushed behind the sofa and peed. Then he wouldn't come out for some time; when he finally did, he was crawling on his stomach and groveling until he had a lot of reassurance. Why did he have an accident, and could we have done anything about it?

IT'S NOT AN ACCIDENT when your puppy pees through apprehension and stress—it's probably your own behavior that needs to be addressed.

A He didn't forget his training: you've got an unusually sensitive puppy, and he was peeing (and groveling) to try to avert your anger. Young dogs sometimes revert to infantile behavior to send the signal that they are desperate to appease you. When a dog pees under stress like this, it's quite an extreme action and should be read as a sign to take his upbringing slowly and gently.

This doesn't mean offering endless reassurance (you want an independent dog, not a clingy, fearful one—and if you go to great lengths to reassure him every time he's frightened you will be sending him a signal that it's OK for him to hide behind you and depend on you like a small puppy, not an adult dog). **Your dog needs kind, consistent, gentle instruction from you in the basics of mannerly behavior.**

Don't raise your voice to him, because this is usually counterproductive in a tense situation. Give him clear directions when you're going through basic training exercises and reinforce his confidence by concentrating on the things he does know and can do easily whenever he seems uncertain. (Can't seem to master the "stay" command? Then return to "sit," and praise him warmly when he gets it right.) Watch his body language; the more easily you can read the first signs of apprehension, the easier you'll find it to give him reassurance in a way he can understand. You'll find more information on body language in the chapters that follow.

IRRITATING, but did he have anything else to chew? Always look at ways to anticipate and prevent unwanted behavior in a pup; it's much easier than correcting it after the event.

SPECIES WATCH

Urinating through nervousness isn't uncommon in young, anxious animals of many species. And animals use urine for other purposes, too. Male goats liberally spray their faces and front legs with their own urine prior to courting a female; their strong and very recognizable scent acts as an aphrodisiac and encourages the female to mate.

Why does my puppy … look guilty when I tell her off?

Q I've been told that dogs don't feel guilt, so I was surprised the other day when my puppy had made (yet another!) puddle and I told her off and wagged a finger at her—and her response was to sit down and hang her head. She may not have been feeling guilty, but she certainly looked as though she was! What was going on?

THE WAGGING FINGER isn't making your dog feel guilty, but it is causing her to become rather nervous: Why are you angry? She's forgotten all about the puddle she made.

A She was reacting to your body language and the disapproving sound of your voice. It's unlikely that guilt came into it; in fact, unless you actually caught her in the act of making the puddle, she would have already forgotten all about it. **Dogs associate only very immediate consequences with their acts—even something that happened just a minute or two before won't be connected in her brain with any correction she receives,** which is why trainers suggest that you correct undesirable actions only as they take place (and always with distraction and positive reinforcement, not punishment). The old custom of rubbing a puppy's nose in her mess to correct her was not only unkind but also pointless: the puppy didn't understand anything except that her owner was angry and that she was afraid. It may even have reinforced the problem behavior. It's important to make sure that she associates you with positive things.

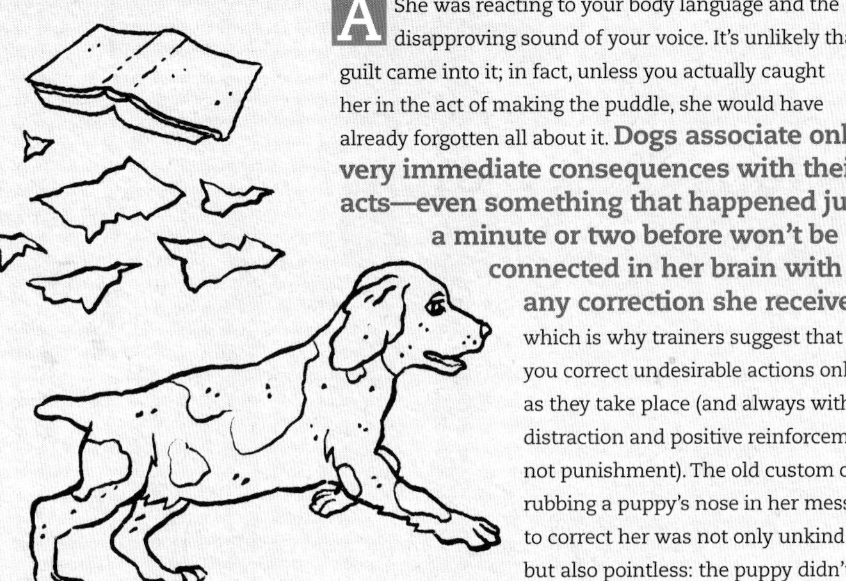

LOOK FOR A REASON Did your puppy make the puddle because she was left a little too long? Or chew the book because she was teething and didn't have anything else to chew?

For dogs, like all species who live socially, humans included, their safety is their priority. So they have evolved a sophisticated sign language (the eminent Norwegian trainer Turid Rugaas first described these as "calming signals") to let those around them know that they themselves do not pose a threat.

An extreme example might involve a dog lying on its back exposing its stomach (message: I pose no threat, I am making myself vulnerable to you). In a more everyday context (an annoyed voice, a raised finger), your puppy decided to lower her head, averting a direct gaze at you, and to sit down, in an effort to calm you down, which in human eyes looks very much like guilt.

Why does my puppy ... only like hard toys?

Q I've always kept dogs and most have had valued parts of familiar bedding or "comfort blankets" through puppyhood (some have even continued to carry them around as adults). My current pup, however, now eight months old, doesn't seem to value anything but the hardest toys—he loves Kong toys, hard rubber bones, and chews, but has never shown any interest in anything soft. Is there any particular reason for this, or is it just a question of different dogs, different preferences?

FOR A SATISFYING CHEW, a puppy with a second set of sharp adult teeth on the way may find hard rubber the most rewarding texture to bite on.

A It probably is a question of different dogs, different preferences, but the breed of dog may also have something to do with it. Although it can be misleading to stereotype dogs within their breeds (many people will have met a surprisingly shy terrier, or a serious-minded retriever, whatever those breeds are "supposed" to be like—most dogs don't seem to have read the manuals), it is often true that retrieving breeds such as spaniels, labradors and golden retrievers seem to love mouthing soft toys and pieces of soft cloth, while groups such as terriers—originally used as hunters rather than retrievers—prefer something with a bit more resistance and "bite."

OFFER A SELECTION of toys and games until your dog's tastes are fully formed; you never know what might be a surprise hit.

There's another factor, too—at eight months, your puppy is still trying out his adult teeth, and **it's between seven and nine months that the second big chewing stage arrives as part of adolescence.** He probably finds harder toys relieve his need to chew more satisfactorily. Don't decide yet that he only likes hard toys: keep his options open. Most dogs arrive at a fixed preference at around one year old. Some are exclusively interested in sticks and balls, while others prefer something that squeaks or makes a noise. Still others like soft fabric toys best—and there are a few all-arounders who simply love any toy at any time.

In the meantime, one great summer treat for a Kong-loving dog who is working his teeth is to cover one open end of the Kong in plastic wrap, pour in some meaty gravy and place it upright in the freezer. When the gravy is frozen, remove the wrap. Your dog will thoroughly enjoy licking out the frozen gravy little by little.

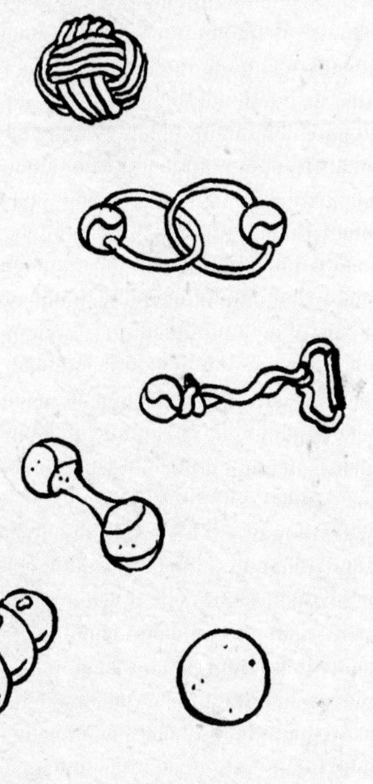

Why does my puppy … need to be carried down the stairs?

Q The breeder who sold us our dachshund puppy was very firm that she should be carried up and downstairs until she was eight or nine months old. We were also told she shouldn't be allowed to jump up on furniture or to play too athletically. She's a lively dog, and my understanding is that dachshunds were originally bred to hunt badgers, so presumably they are quite tough—is it really necessary to be so gentle with her?

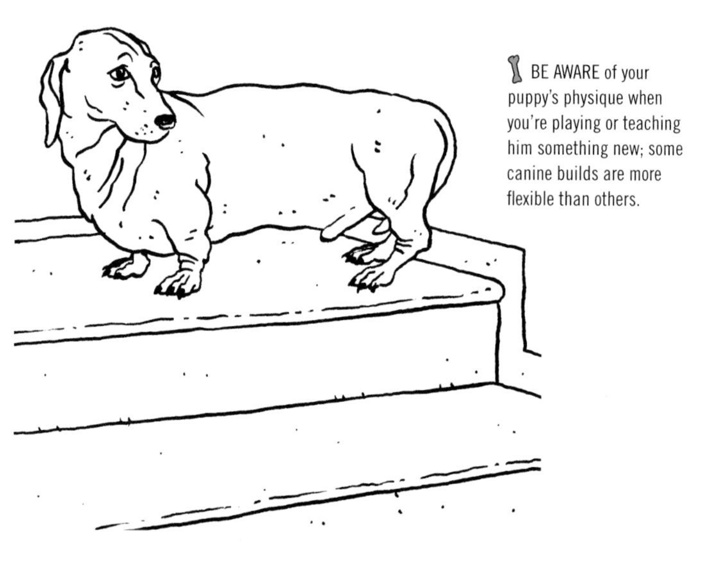

BE AWARE of your puppy's physique when you're playing or teaching him something new; some canine builds are more flexible than others.

SPECIES WATCH

Specialist breeding isn't new, although the variety of dog designs that it's produced is remarkable. No other animal can boast such variety under the umbrella of a single species, although breeding for special characteristics in domesticated animals has had some surprising results, including—in Britain—a breeding program for miniature pigs that weigh in at less than a fifth of the porcine average.

A The short answer is "yes." If an experienced and responsible breeder gives you advice like this, you should listen. But there's a longer explanation, too, which has to do with specialization within breeds.

If dogs were bred without the benefit of human intervention, they would eventually all end up at around the same size and weight. The original, basic dog of no particular breed weighs in at a compact 30–35 pounds and comes in a neat, practical design.

But dogs are an unusual species in that breeding to emphasize some features and reduce or eliminate others, has produced an extraordinarily wide range of "designs," some far more practical than others. In some breeds, features have become particularly exaggerated over the last 50 or so years, now that fewer dogs are bred to do their original jobs and more because... well, just because humans like the way they look.

Dachs is German for badger—and hunting badgers is just what this little dog was bred for (anyone who has ever faced down a determined dachshund will vouch for its strength of character). The strong, low build was helpful to dogs who often hunted below ground, but gradually appearance took over and today's very long dachshund back can be prone to slipped disks and other problems. As a result, the dogs need to be introduced to stairs carefully and shouldn't be allowed to make a habit of jumping. It's also important to keep a dachshund's weight under control, because extra pounds will put additional strain on the spine.

DOG BREEDING has led to an astounding variety of specialization; no other species comes in such a wide range of "finishes."

Why has my puppy ... become so naughty?

Q We have an eight-month-old puppy who has proved easy to train. Recently, however, we acquired a six-year-old dog from a rescue association, who is a lovely, placid dog; she has settled in well, and plays good-humoredly with the puppy. However, the puppy has suddenly become really naughty, and seems to have forgotten everything he's learned. Our new dog is not leading him astray—why is he behaving like this?

THE RELAXED DEMEANOR of an older dog may sometimes encourage a younger one to experiment with the status quo of his particular domestic pack.

A The status quo in the household has changed at the time in which your puppy is an adolescent Having another dog around may have made him more conscious of status—and her permissive demeanor has encouraged him to decide to enhance his place in the pecking order. **Any canine addition to or subtraction from the family will always make some difference, and it can be fascinating to watch dogs working out who comes first in which situation.** They seem to be variously conscious of and worried by status, but they all have some awareness of it, and it's hard to anticipate what shift in canine politics will provoke a change in behavior. You may also have influenced the situation unconsciously by disciplining your puppy a little less simply because you now have two dogs, one of whom is invariably well behaved.

If you want your puppy to go back to his well-behaved best, you need to assert yourself over both dogs. Although only the puppy's behavior needs tightening up, the message you will be sending is that you are the leader of this pack, and that both dogs need to follow your guidance.

In this way, you can use the good manners of your rescue dog as a reinforcement, rather than letting her good temper become a reason for your puppy to walk all over her. Go back to starter training if necessary, enlisting the older dog to show the younger how it's done. Keep the sessions lighthearted and fun, so that both dogs look forward to them.

MOST DOGS FIND IT REASSURING to understand that they are all members of the pack under the supervision of a leader who gives clear and firm direction—you.

Why has my puppy… begun to guard her food so fiercely?

Q Our puppy has a good appetite and has always eaten his meals quickly and enthusiastically. In the last month, though, he's begun to wolf down his food as though he's starving, and—an extremely unwelcome development—once or twice he's growled when someone has passed close to him as he's eating. He's just hit the seven-month stage—why is he doing this, and should I be concerned about this new behavior?

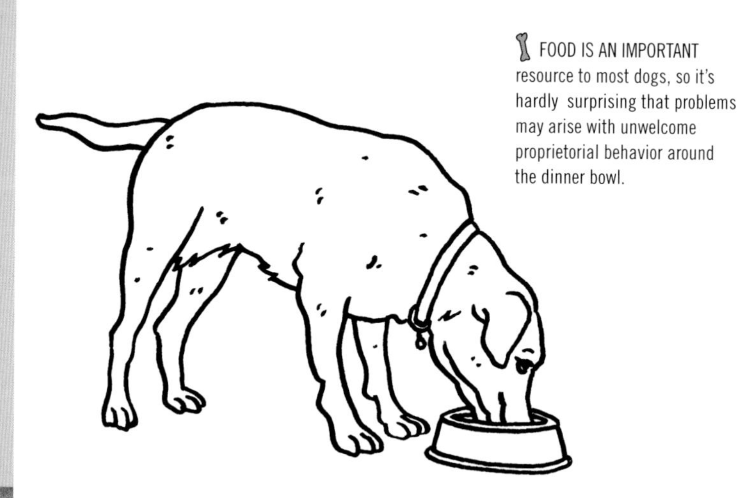

FOOD IS AN IMPORTANT resource to most dogs, so it's hardly surprising that problems may arise with unwelcome proprietorial behavior around the dinner bowl.

A Yes, you should—a little. The experts call this behavior "resource guarding" (the dog is feeling possessive about what's his and is prepared to give you a strong warning not to move in on it), and it's a sign that rules should be firmed up.

Your dog is hitting his teenage stage, and it sounds as though he's picked this unwelcome way to assert himself. The last thing you want is for him to become more defensive around his food; the growl is a warning, and you should never push your dog into acting on it—from his point of view he has given you fair warning not to come closer, and if you ignore him, he might feel compelled to follow it up by snapping.

Many owners will consult a trainer or behaviorist to help them through problems with guarding while their pet is still a puppy; it can be helpful to have expert advice before the unwanted behavior becomes a habit.

A PUPPY MAY TEST HIS PACK ranking by approaching an older dog's food, but this is one experiment that is likely to win him an uncompromising lesson in both manners and status.

Resource guarding can often be overcome by using exchange. If every time he gives up something, he gets both a treat and the original resource returned to him, your pup will understand that it's worth giving up something in the short term, and his trust in the person with whom he's exchanging will be reinforced. Dog behaviorists use this principle with all sorts of unwanted guarding behavior. Another way it can be prevented from developing around the food bowl with very young puppies is to put only a small amount of food in the bowl at first, then add to it little by little while the pup is eating. In this way, he will get used to having humans around his food, but for a very positive reason.

Why does my puppy … get tired so quickly?

Q Our new puppy seems to tire easily—she takes long naps during the day, as well as sleeping for surprisingly long periods at night. She's friendly and outgoing and our children love her, but she can't play with them for very long before she goes in her basket and has a nap. She came to us two weeks ago at eight weeks old; her breeder told us about the importance to her of having a cozy place she feels safe, and she obviously loves her basket, but she seems to spend an awful lot of time in it. Is there something wrong?

LIKE SMALL CHILDREN, a young puppy can fall asleep suddenly—sometimes almost mid-activity.

Assuming that you had her checked over thoroughly by the vet when she first arrived, she's probably just...tired! Canine youngsters, like human ones, are working hard in every imaginable way through those first few months. Not only does your pup have a lot of physical growing to do, but she also has completely new surroundings to get used to, a family to learn to get along with, and some kids to exhaust her, too. And puppies tend to give every activity their all, playing, eating, exploring and meeting new people and animals all with 100 percent interest and enthusiasm—a large part of why they're quite so appealing to humans—which quickly uses up a considerable amount of energy.

A NEW WORLD TO EXPLORE
With a lot of growing to do, your pup may find life gets exhausting.

You may also be the owner of a dog who's going to grow up to be naturally mellow. She's outgoing and good tempered with the children, but time to rest and recharge the batteries is key in this age group. **If you have a puppy who knows when she's tired, rather than one who gets exhausted and eventually cranky because she's so into everything, that's a big advantage, just as it would be having a baby who is an untroubled sleeper.** If you're still worried, mention the tiredness at her next vet's exam; he will probably be quick to reassure you.

And when your puppy makes it clear that she does want to sleep, let her go to her basket or into her crate without letting the children hassle her for another few minutes' play—her "safe place" should be just that: a place where, when she needs to nap, she can do so in peace.

SPECIES WATCH

How much sleep an animal takes varies enormously. Large, land-grazing mammals such as elephants and giraffes sleep comparatively little, because the nutritional content of their diet means that they have to eat almost continually and don't have time to sleep for prolonged periods. Many birds literally sleep with one eye open, dozing with only part of their brain, while the other part stays alert for nearby danger.

Why does my puppy ... turn her head away if another dog approaches?

Q Our puppy has never been a particularly confident dog, but we made sure that he met lots of other dogs (pre-vetted and friendly) from when we first had him at eight weeks. He still hangs back when he meets a new dog; he used to roll over on his back but now, at 12 weeks, he stands his ground as an unfamiliar dog approaches, but turns his head away. He's comfortable with dogs he knows, but the head-turning persists over the first few meetings. Why does he do this?

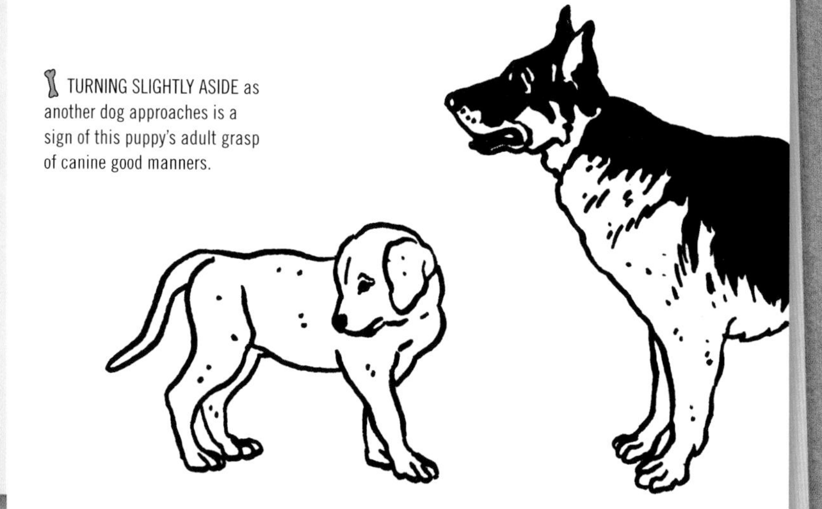

TURNING SLIGHTLY ASIDE as another dog approaches is a sign of this puppy's adult grasp of canine good manners.

A He does it because he is being careful and polite. The fact that your puppy no longer rolls over but remains standing as he's introduced to another dog is a sign that he's growing up—**young puppies tend to roll over and expose their bellies to make it clear that they are unthreatening; it's an "appeasing" gesture intended to pacify anyone unfamiliar who may be uncertain of the puppy's role.** As he gains in confidence, he feels able to stand his ground but is still deferring to an approaching dog in a controlled way. He is avoiding making direct eye contact (which can be perceived as a challenge when dogs meet) but is remaining in place and allowing the other dog to approach. If he is wagging his tail easily, he is probably feeling quite confident; if he looks a bit too stiff, he may be feeling a little nervous. The more enjoyable experiences he has when meeting other dogs, the easier he will feel socially.

Adult dogs who are meeting a regular playmate on equal terms may approach each other in a bouncy way, give a perfunctory sniff to the face (not usually head-on), and then launch into a play bow, with rear end in the air, tail waving, and front end lowered with paws extended. More formal introductions usually start with a rear sniff, move on to a brief facial examination, then both dogs may part, play, or remain, friendly but neutral, in each other's proximity. Your puppy has learned that he can send a signal to an approaching dog that is likely to make the forthcoming encounter an amiable one.

PUPPIES WHO ARE PRESUMPTUOUS with older dogs are risking being taught a sharp lesson in respect.

Chapter two

A dog's-eye view

Sometimes the answer to a particular question of canine behavior might be general (all dogs do that...), sometimes it might be breed specific (this breed is hardwired to do that...), and frequently they're absolutely dog specific (Snoopy does that because... he's a very special dog—the secret conviction of all dog owners everywhere). **In this section, we mainly look at doggy behavior that is all dog—the stuff that you really can't identify with, no matter how much you try.** Opinions among the experts are in any case divided as to how much we understand about the way dogs think and whether they have a definite sense of self, for example. However hard we try, we're humans, not dogs, so we can only interpret from our own biased species' viewpoint. But there certainly are some activities and actions that are all dog, and which dogs have inherited down an extremely long genetic line.

Why does my dog ... butt-sniff every dog we meet in the park?

Q My dog introduces himself to every dog we see in the park—but always from the rear end. I know this is fairly standard dog behavior (although he seems to engage in it more than most!), but I want to know why he never starts a meeting face to face? Surely there's as much information to be exchanged with the front end as with the back?

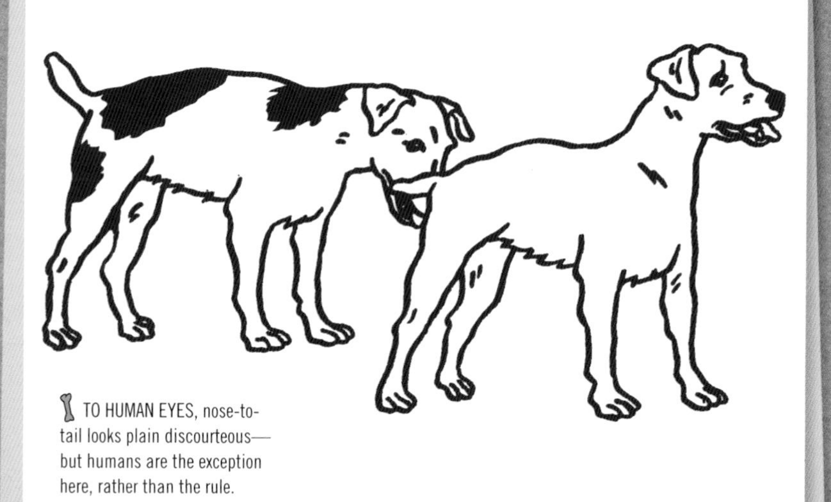

TO HUMAN EYES, nose-to-tail looks plain discourteous—but humans are the exception here, rather than the rule.

It may look intimate to you, but to a dog, it's infinitely more polite to offer a modest butt-sniff by way of an introduction than to come up boldly face-to-face. The rudest way you can meet a dog is with direct eye contact. **Humans, brought up to meet a glance directly and to extend their hand, don't usually understand the typical canine introduction. Dogs learn a lot from sniffing a new acquaintance's rear end, because of the scent glands situated there.** As a dog's sense of smell is more than 44 times stronger than ours (see page 23), it's unsurprising that your dog will go by his nose rather than starting up a facial conversation.

FACE TO FACE ... but think of it as stage two of the conversation.

If you watch a selection of dogs meeting, you'll notice that some are considerably more polite with their introductory butt-sniff than others. A polite, well-socialized dog will approach from the side, sniff briefly, and move on, often approaching the other's face slightly sideways on, making it clear that he isn't being confrontational. A rude dog will move in intrusively, sniff long and hard, and sometimes even go in for a full inguinal sniff (the polite term for a thorough nasal examination of the other's genitals).

A rude introduction doesn't usually pay off, however —most dogs will move away from it, rather than turning slightly to accept an approach face-to-face. Dogs don't look each other directly in the eye until they are quite familiar, and you'll rarely see prolonged eye contact even with dogs who are good friends. If you were comparing dog introductions with human ones, then you could interpret the rear sniff as the handshake, the how-do-you-do, and the brief conversation in which you both establish key facts about yourselves, whereas the subsequent nose-to-nose encounter takes things on to the next stage.

SPECIES WATCH

You may have thought that dogs had an unusual way of approaching one another, but in fact, humans are one of the exceptions in this respect rather than the rule. Far more mammals effect their introductions nose-to-rear than face-to-face—elephants are also an exception to this, introducing each other trunk-to-trunk, and most monkeys rely on facial expression to know whether it's safe to approach one another or not.

Why does my dog ... turn in circles before she goes to sleep?

Q My dog has a padded bed of which she is especially fond—she will drag it around the house in hot or cold weather seeking out the most temperature-appropriate spot to settle down for the night. After she's had her final constitutional, she leaps into the basket and rakes it around with her paws, as though she were digging. As soon as all the stuffing in the cushion has been redistributed (and it looks thoroughly uncomfortable to me), she circles in time-honored dog fashion, settles down, and goes to sleep. I've heard all sorts of explanations for both the digging and the circling—why does she do it?

ELABORATE CANINE rituals may not all have their roots in the family life that your dog lives today.

A There's no absolutely definitive answer to this one: as you say, there are various different explanations, all of which can be argued persuasively. The most traditional one for the circling is that wild dogs settle down to sleep in long grass and turn in circles to create a comfortable bed for themselves before lying down. **Other explanations claim that the dog is checking his environs for threats (insects, snakes, the smell of other predators), and getting a 360-degree view of his surroundings before he settles, or that he is sniffing for the direction of the prevailing wind so that he can sleep with his nose in it—so that he will smell the approach of anything that is dangerous to him long before it arrives.** You can accept any or all of these; the circling behavior is shared by wolves (although wolf cubs, just like puppies, sleep in a heap to maximize body warmth and a feeling of security; as they mature they will begin to sleep alone, and circle just as dogs do), which indicates that it ties into the animals' basic instincts for survival.

SOME OF THE UNFAMILIAR aspects of domestic dogs' behavior may go all the way back to the time when dog packs lived in the wild.

There's a simple but persuasive explanation advanced for the raking and digging—animals sometimes do this in hot countries before settling down in order to displace the sun-warmed top layer of earth and reach cooler dirt beneath. As the action you describe sounds similar to that of a dog digging under a shady bush on a hot day before flopping down in the space he has made, the most likely answer is that this is a piece of pure instinct; something that your dog "just has to do" before she can settle.

Why does my dog ... scrabble up the earth after he urinates?

Q I have an intact male dog who is five years old. We've always lived in open countryside, so he mostly walks off the leash. When we go out for his first morning walk, one of his first jobs is to find somewhere secluded and comfortable to relieve himself—and, as soon as he's done so, he stretches out his body and, with his back legs, exuberantly scrabbles up the dirt in long channels, scratching it up with his claws. As soon as he's finished, he joins me and continues his walk. What is he doing, and why?

"I WAS HERE" is the most significant way that a dog can leave a reminder of who he is to those who walk by later.

A Dogs know that they're vulnerable when they eliminate—for just a minute, your dog is crouching and he's at a disadvantage. You've probably noticed that when any dog is off-leash, they pick their spot with care—not too near to anyone else, and often backed by a bush or tree, so that no one can sneak up on them.

After the deed's done, however, your dog has a second job to do, and that's the explanation for the energetic scrabbling. He's distributing his scent as broadly as he can, to let other dogs know who he is and that he was there. When your dog defecates, he simultaneously exudes a minute amount of oil from the anal sacs that are located at each side of his rectum. The glands are pea-sized and unless you've ever had a dog who had problems with retention of fluid there, you may never have noticed them. But they're a key part of your dog's anatomy, because the oily liquid inside them not only offers a slight lubrication that makes it easier for your dog to defecate, but also gives him his absolutely unique smell: as separate and identifiable between dogs as fingerprints are in humans. And, as we know, smell is extremely important to dogs.

When your dog has spread his scent, he kicks vigorously backward to ensure that he's marked as wide an area as possible. Not only is he letting other dogs know that he's been by, he's also leaving as strong an impression as he can. We can't know whether, at a conscious level, he's thinking, "The wider I spread my scent, the larger and more important all the other dogs will think I am," but most human onlookers would agree that a dog trotting happily away from his scent marker gives off the distinct air of a "good job, well done."

"MEDIUM-SIZED, fully functional" is what canine passersby will read in the message left by your dog.

SPECIES WATCH

Tree-dwelling monkeys can't scrabble in the same way a dog does, but some species will disseminate their scent in a different way: the capuchin monkey, for instance, urinates onto its palms and the soles of its feet, then rubs its scent along branches as it climbs, leaving just as strong a signal in the trees as a dog does on the ground.

Why does my dog …
roll in anything stinky?

Q I've lived with dogs of lots of different breeds all my life, from Afghan hounds to terriers, and probably almost the only thing that they have all had in common is their enjoyment of rolling in something that smells disgusting. It might be fox scat, it might be something dead, or it might be something completely unidentifiable—every single dog I've ever had has followed this pattern and, apparently, they only roll in things that, to humans, smell revolting. Why?

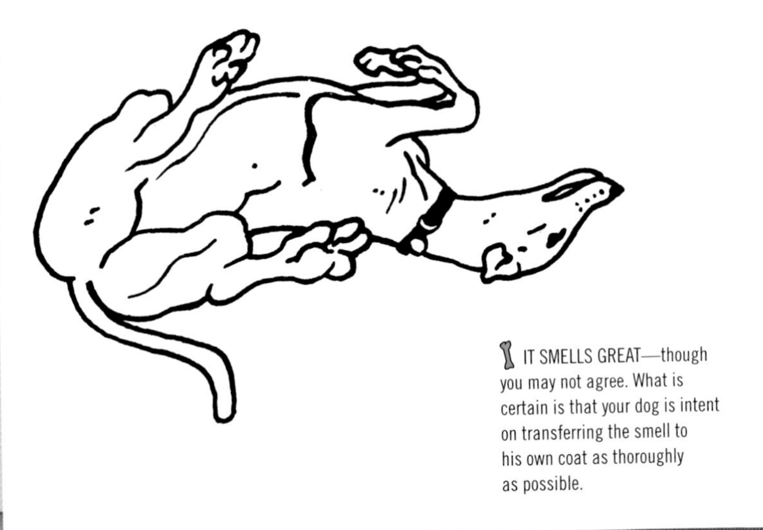

IT SMELLS GREAT—though you may not agree. What is certain is that your dog is intent on transferring the smell to his own coat as thoroughly as possible.

A There are several options put forward by behavior experts for this one: no definitive answer, but quite a lot of interesting possibilities. When wolves were observed rolling in something smelly, researchers studying their behavior initially believed that they were masking their own smell so as to confuse any potential prey, who wouldn't immediately smell "wolf" but a mixed bouquet of scents including, one must assume, decomposing possum, too.

Two alternative explanations for the rolling have also been advanced—as far as wolves go, that is—with the first suggesting that the roller is going to take the scent of his find back to the pack, "advertising" what he's found to the others; and the second, probably even less appetizing, that the roller may be marking the carrion he's found with his own smell, declaring ownership over it. Neither of these holds up under argument and yet another idea suggests that both wolves and dogs roll in foul-smelling goop purely because they love the scent.

This last suggestion may not be as far-fetched as it appears when you consider that the most expensive scents that humans apply to themselves have traditionally contained some decidedly organic ingredients (spermaceti oil, musk, and so on). We think they smell delicious, but most dogs wouldn't agree with that any more than their humans would luxuriate in eau de skunk. **The scent-masking and purely-for-enjoyment ideas seem the most likely options for anyone who has seen the expression of a dog rolling in something foul and identified it, in human terms, as radiating pure, unalloyed pleasure.**

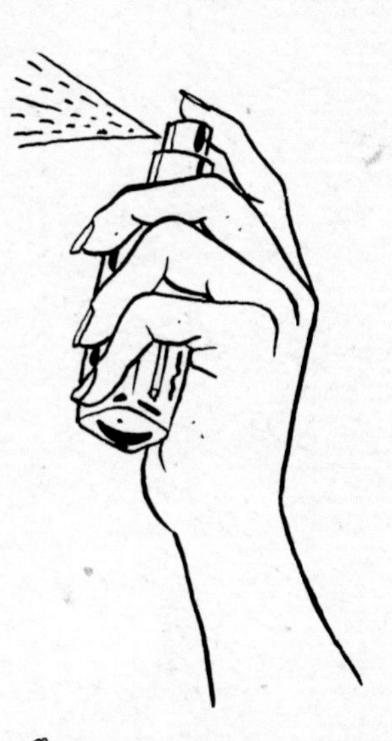

BEFORE YOU JUDGE, consider the ingredients of your own favorite perfume. Are dogs really any stranger than humans?

Why does my dog ... never get into a group game right away?

Q My dog isn't generally shy or retreating: she's eager and playful, both with humans and with visiting dogs on her own turf. In fact, if you saw her at home, you'd say that she loved other dogs. But out in the park it's a different story. If we meet a group of dogs playing together, she will often hide behind me and act as if she's fearful, peeking out and looking worried. This only lasts for a minute or two; eventually she'll come out and, after five minutes or so, she'll join in with the play and apparently enjoy herself. But what does this sudden shyness mean?

CAUTION PAYS OFF, so it's sensible to size up the structure of a game—who's "it" and who's top dog—before launching right in.

A The fearful behavior is most likely to have arisen from one of two causes: either an obvious one—your dog likes the familiar and feels that things aren't within her control when she's away from home turf, or something less obvious—some incident that you would have considered trivial and may not even have noticed has upset her and she's attached it specifically to playing in the park.

Often, owners describe their dogs as "suddenly deciding" that they dislike or are afraid of something, but in reality dogs don't usually make these decisions for no reason. Their rationale tends to differ from the human way of thinking in which part of the incident they associate with trauma.

Say your dog had a small scrap with a large black dog at the park. It was brief; to your eyes it looked like a minor incident, and there wasn't any physical damage, but your dog was badly frightened, though only for a moment, and she's attached the problem to playing in the park rather than to large black dogs, or even that dog in particular, as a person would be likely to do. So there is a rational basis to what looks like irrational behavior.

How to convince a dog who has decided that a situation is scary that the situation is actually safe? Petting and encouragement don't usually help—to the canine mind, this will confirm that there's a reason to be frightened. Instead, behave as calmly and confidently as possible yourself. That way, you'll send her a message that everything is fine; you're not making a fuss about any threat, so there's probably nothing to be frightened of. She obviously loves to play, so she may well overcome her fear, given a little time and a few more enjoyable games with canine friends.

Why does my male dog … always pee after my female dog?

Q I have two Jack Russell terriers, a three-year-old female and a four-year-old male. When they're let out after being indoors for a while, I've noticed that the dog seems to wait to relieve himself until after the female squats to pee, then rushes over and lifts his leg directly over where she has just been. Why does he do this, and would he do it if my other dog were male?

IN THE CANINE WORLD, he who pees last is sending important messages about his standing to those who come after him.

A He's instinctively using his urine to overmark hers. Any owner waiting outdoors on a freezing night for several dogs to go through their peeing ritual will have noticed that urination can seem quite a complex business for dogs. **Dogs often overmark each other's urine and to the onlooker the "contest" to see who gets to mark the spot last can be quite amusing. For the dog, though, peeing is a serious subject.**

He can use his pee to mark his territory, leave important information about himself to those who follow him, and to overlay the pee of others, either to "claim" them (often the case when a male overmarks a female) or simply to leave his mark last, and therefore most prominently to those who may pass by and sniff when he's left the spot.

Whether or not your dog would overmark if your other dog were male would depend on their relative status within your household, and how status-conscious the dogs were. Some dogs seem very conscious of and concerned about their standing within their pack—those in their household—while others seem comparatively laid back about the pecking order. A female, equally, may overmark a dog's mark, although her physical limitations make it harder if the dog has cocked his leg on a tree or hydrant. It's not an insurmountable difficulty though; in a few cases, females who are highly status conscious have been recorded lifting their leg in the same way as a male dog in order to hit exactly the right spot and leave their own mark as the final one in the sequence.

"I THINK IT WAS A LARGE DOG"—we can't know exactly what information dogs leave for the next passerby on trees and fire hydrants, but every dog coming along afterward will "read" it with interest, and sometimes add their own notes.

Why does my dog … not play nicely in a group?

Q I have a Belgian Malinois sheepdog who has just turned two. We socialized him carefully while he was still a puppy, but he still seems uneasy playing in a group. He joins in, but if you watch him closely the role that he seems to take up is much more like that of a policeman overseeing the game than a participant. As soon as two dogs are interacting happily together, he will barge in to break it up, but he doesn't appear to want to play himself. Why does he do this? Is it just his personality coming out, or is it something we could have caught and prevented while he was still a puppy?

PLAY WORKS BEST when the participating dogs aren't too status conscious to relax into the game.

A You're an excellent observer of dog behavior, and what you describe is typical of a young, rather anxious, and very status-conscious dog. The likelihood is that he wants to be in charge of the situation but he doesn't have the natural seniority, confidence, and status to attract the deference he longs for. And since he can't control the whole picture, he breaks up the play instead. He's an alpha wannabe, and these can be some of the hardest dogs for owners to "teach" to relax.

In the past, it was believed that the original wolf pack from which dogs derived had a single leader and there was constant conflict over status. More recent studies have found that wolves actually enjoy a very high degree of social cooperation within the pack, with individuals usually taking up the role for which they're best suited. Fighting is much rarer than humans, with their idea of wolves as "wild" animals, might assume.

Dogs, equally, are well versed in the niceties, and in the course of a play session you can observe all kinds of exchanges, from pursuer to pursued and from top dog to underdog. It's probable that your pet finds all this too important to enjoy a game—he can't relax, because in play another dog might challenge him. So, like the nervous child who starts bullying, he appoints himself bossy overseer of the game.

Wannabe dogs are often relieved when a human takes charge. The best way for you to put a stop to the unwanted policeman behavior may be to provide a distraction and establish your control overall; for example, try lining them up to sit for a treat.

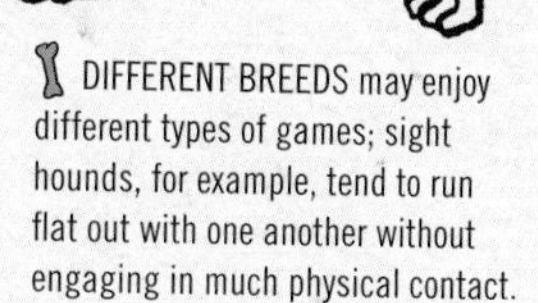

DIFFERENT BREEDS may enjoy different types of games; sight hounds, for example, tend to run flat out with one another without engaging in much physical contact.

SPECIES WATCH

Aspiring middle managers of any species may find life more difficult than either pack leaders or animals who are content with their status. A study of dwarf mongooses found that these little animals have highly developed systems for deciding who rises to power in each group. But because there were firm "rules," the animals seemed to suffer less stress than in species where each individual had to fight to gain status.

Why does my dog ... sit down when another dog approaches?

Q I have a young retriever—she's almost three—who tends to be slightly shy. The other retrievers we meet are exuberant, but she defies breed stereotyping; she hates to be bounced at by young dogs and she prefers rather staid play with a few dogs who are older than her and sedate in their behavior. When she sees an unfamiliar dog, she sits down (we've never asked her to do this, so it seems to be instinctive). Sometimes she'll even go into a full lie. Why does she do this? If the other dog seems friendly, she'll get up after a moment or two and they'll go through an introduction—but what is the sit for?

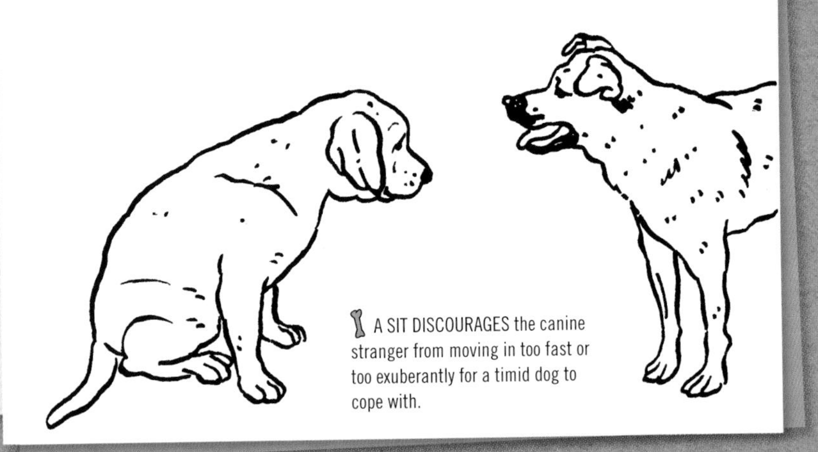

A SIT DISCOURAGES the canine stranger from moving in too fast or too exuberantly for a timid dog to cope with.

A Your dog is naturally a fairly cautious character and she prefers a quiet life. She sits down because it's one of the time-honored "calming" signals that seem to be recognized by all dogs. Young and enthusiastic dogs will often concertina the introductory stages of the canine conversation and go into a play bow (a signal all dog owners would recognize, with the rear raised and the front paws flat on the ground), which is an invitation to another dog to play.

Your dog is sending the opposite: a slow-down signal. In the same way as when a dog turns aside to sniff the ground, or yawns, or sits down to scratch in a slightly surprising context (see pages 10–11), **she's using body language that tends to calm a situation down, and gives her time to prepare for an introduction to the approaching dog.**

Some experts claim that dogs recognize different types and associate them with "typical" behaviors; that is, they, like you, may see a retriever and associate the dog's appearance with especially lively play. If this really is the case (and it's a theory, not proven behavior) then your dog may be the subject of more bouncy play approaches than some other breeds, and the sitting or even lying response is her way of letting others know that however she looks, she prefers her play sedate! If she remains calm and doesn't look frightened or stressed—check for tension in her face, because a scared dog will usually close its mouth and get a "tight" look around the muzzle—she is simply demonstrating that she is socially savvy and can deal with her natural shyness.

HAS SHE REALLY FOUND an interesting smell, or is she just showing a proper sense of caution in the face of unknown dogs approaching?

Why does my dog … "point" with his paw when he sees something he wants to chase?

Q I have a mixed-breed rescue dog and we're not too sure about his origins. He's quite rangy; he looks like a mixture between a greyhound and a heavier hound-type dog. He keenly chases anything small and furry, although he's never been fast enough to catch the rabbits and squirrels he targets. What we notice most is that, whenever he sees anything in the distance that he'd like to chase, he "freezes" in position and lifts one paw, just like a trained hunting dog. Is this instinctive behavior, or is it some kind of indicator of his breeding?

INSTINCT OR BREEDING? We can't be sure of its origins, but the long paw lift certainly seems to be part of the hardwiring of many hunting breeds.

HUNTING ALERT! Lowering the front body and raising the rear isn't always preparation for play. Some dogs "alert" like this just before chasing their prey.

A Opinions vary a little on this one. Most dogs have a natural paw lift which they use in all sorts of situations. Some may lift a paw when they're a little uncertain—for example, you might see a tentative lift in a dog who is just about to greet another he hasn't met before. At other times, it seems to be used as an placatory gesture, particularly when it's directed toward a dog's owner. And the paw lift is also seen in dogs who are looking at something that's arousing their interest.

It's this last use that probably developed the long paw lift that hunting dogs show. Some experts claim that a pointing dog is acting instinctively, but holds the paw longer and stiller than the average, because he's intensely focused and gearing himself for action. Others claim that the behavior has been trained into hunting dogs over the centuries so that, when a dog spots prey, he freezes and focuses on it hard, giving the hunters enough time to make a shot. **A dog who had a natural "point" would have stood a greater chance of being used for breeding, so that pointing became a natural characteristic of certain breeds of working dog.**

Whether you believe that it's purely instinctive behavior or something that owes a little to human interference, the original paw lift is seen at some time or other in almost every dog breed, from terriers to toys and spaniels to schipperkes—and dogs who have never been on the hunting field can sometimes hold the pose for a surprisingly long time—so it seems most likely that training and breeding have adapted an instinctive and natural behavior to a human purpose.

SPECIES WATCH

Sophisticated hunting behavior occurs in the vast majority of preying species. Trapdoor spiders set elaborately camouflaged ambushes for their minute prey, while chimpanzees have been observed using tools to help them in their hunt for bushbabies and other small animals. In research, the learned behavior of the chimpanzee is seen as more highly developed than the instinctive behavior of the spider.

Why does my smart dog ... have problems with some basic training?

Q I'm in the process of training my mixed-breed dog (she's seven months old) and we've been having difficulties with a couple of specific signals. If I stand and call her to "come" she stands stock still, but if I turn to walk away, she rushes up to me. Similarly, with "stay," she'll move toward me, even now, when we've been practicing for weeks. We haven't had any problems with other verbal signals, and she's keen to learn and seems to enjoy training sessions. What is going on?

DOGS NATURALLY TEND to follow someone who is walking away from them, and this can be a help when you're teaching them to "come."

A Dogs don't rely on the meaning of words in the way humans do—or at least we don't believe they do. A dog who is trying to learn what you want her to do is listening to your voice, looking at your expression, reading your body posture, and wondering what she needs to do to get the chicken treat all at the same time. **And because dogs are sensitive to the tiniest details of body language, it may be that your body seems to her to contradict the signals you're giving with your voice.**

Ask someone else to watch you both while you run through the commands your dog knows, including the two that are causing problems (they can sit quietly on the sidelines). Maybe you're moving your body in the same way with every signal, and your dog is getting confused; maybe you change stance slightly when you come to a signal that you're worried about, so that your dog's picking up your uncertainty about it.

Incidentally, to teach "come," don't stand facing your dog, asking her to walk toward you. She'll find it easier when it's associated with the idea of following you. Try the "come" command as you turn and move away; if she comes with you, you've achieved your goal.

LEANING TOWARD A DOG with your body moving into her space is more likely to encourage her to stay where she is than to come toward you. Add an outstretched hand to the mix, and she's almost certain to stay put.

Why does my dog … sometimes turn a game into a fight?

Q My dog enjoys chasing and play-wrestling with other dogs and plays very energetically. But sometimes he seems to get too intense about playing and the situation turns into a fight. Although it's never had a serious outcome, I still worry about it. Is it possible to tell in advance when this is going to happen and, if so, is there any way that I can stop it before the actual scrimmage breaks out?

IT STARTS AS A GAME But some dogs get so excited that they neglect to tone down their body language.

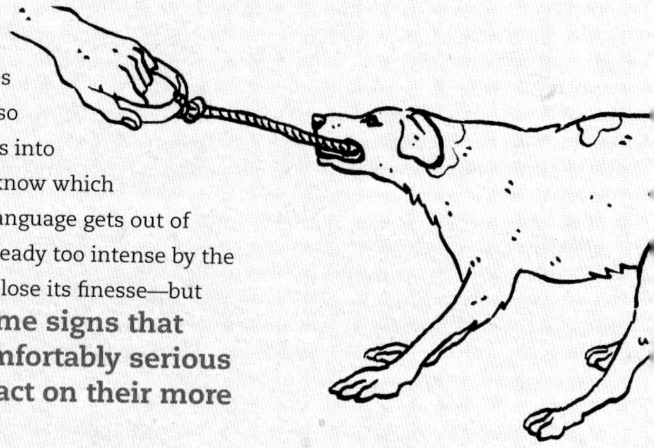

A Dogs who are particularly excitable in play sometimes become overstimulated; they're so focused on the game that it turns into something else. We don't really know which comes first—whether the body language gets out of hand, or whether the game is already too intense by the time the body language starts to lose its finesse—but **you can usually read some signs that things are getting uncomfortably serious before the dogs start to act on their more aggressive impulses.**

TUG-OF-WAR GAMES can be fun—but they're still best avoided with a dog who tends to forget he is playing.

If it tends to be your dog that ramps up the aggression, the first clue you'll see may be in the body language of her playmate. Dogs read each other's nuances fast, and the first to feel uncomfortable with the strength of feeling your dog is expressing will be the dog he's playing with. The dog's body may seem longer and closer to the ground, his mouth may close, and you may notice ridges of tension around his cheeks and eyes.

If your dog is getting into a state of overstimulation, you'll read some of the same signs: his face will tighten and you may see stress ridges on his cheeks and around his forehead. His mouth may be closed—relaxed dogs tend to have open, happy mouths—and his tail and body may get a slightly frozen look in the seconds between the different feints of the game.

The easiest way to deal with all this is to create a diversion as soon as you notice any tense signs. Don't wait to see if it leads to anything; call your dog to you right away and distract him with a toy, a treat, or a moment or two of downtime. Make sure you break up the situation the second you notice any danger signs and you may find he learns more self-control over time. At the least you'll be confident that you can stop things from escalating into a serious fight.

Why does my dog ... need to go to socialization classes?

Q I have five dogs (we live on a farm), but a knowledgeable friend recommended that I take the fifth—our newest recruit, a rescue dog aged eight months—to socialization classes. Won't the other dogs in the household be enough to socialize him? He gets along well with them all and has settled in happily, and the whole pack gets lots of exercise and stimulation. Does he really need more socialization than he's getting as part of daily life?

A GOOD RELATIONSHIP with several dogs at home will make your dog happy in his day-to-day life—but it won't help him to deal with the unexpected.

A It's a good idea. But even a socialization class, while useful, won't answer the full need. What your pup is getting now is a broad experience of home life, but it won't necessarily show him how to cope with the unexpected—what he's learning is that "normal" is a life on a farm with four other dogs. That's a pretty great life for a dog, but if at any time in the future he needs to cope with something different, the best way to prepare him is to expose him to as many experiences as possible, not just a wide range of other dogs, but also unfamiliar noises, sights, and people.

SOCIALIZATION CLASSES introduce pups to a whole range of other dogs, and broaden their experiences, too.

Socialization classes will teach him that there's a canine life beyond that of his particular pack, and will help him to hone his body language. Other experiences will help him to tackle whatever life offers with the same cheerful confidence that he brings to his day-to-day existence.

There's another factor, too, and that's his "rescue" status. Because you can never be quite sure of the life a rescue dog led before you adopted him, it's good to expose him to a lot of scenarios to check that there aren't any deep-seated fears lurking. For example, a dog that used to be left tied up and unexercised in a noisy scrapyard might be fine in a country home, but react explosively to industrial-scale loud noises. It always helps to know your dog's strengths as well as his limitations.

SPECIES WATCH

The young of many animals and birds depend on their parents to teach them what it is to belong to their species, and how to be an owl, a cat, or a bear. Among reptiles, some species of crocodiles offer their young the most extensive care; some even cooperate so that groups of young are cared for in crocodile "nurseries" by one responsible adult while the others go out to "work," hunting.

Why does my dog ... constantly have her hackles up?

Q I have a young and excitable German shepherd. She plays with other dogs enthusiastically, but other owners have sometimes pointed out that when she's socializing in a group or playing with another dog, the ridge of hair at her neck and down the center of her back is almost constantly raised. I thought dogs only raised their hackles when they were going to fight, but she's never fought and she gets along well with the dogs she meets, so why does she do this?

RAISED HACKLES merely confirm that a dog is excited; they don't give you any indication of what he's excited about.

A She's excited and aroused to the point at which the hair is literally standing up on the back of her neck. The degree and frequency with which a dog raises her hackles depends on the individual dog. With some, you hardly ever see the telltale crest at the back of their neck. Others seem to be permanently and literally on a hair trigger, ready to get excited by whatever's going on. While it's true that a stressed dog might raise its hackles as a sign of an undesirable intensity, your description sounds like a dog who is so entranced in the company of other dogs that her whole body is responding.

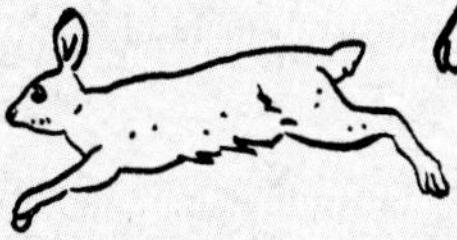

Raised hackles by themselves are simply an indicator of level of intensity, not a signal as to its type. The idea that you would see them only in aggressive dogs isn't accurate; hackles can be raised in dogs who are highly stimulated for any reason at all. Look at the rest of the body language for some other useful clues. **When raised hackles are joined with a relaxed, open, cheerful-looking mouth and a "loose" face, along with a freely sweeping tail, your dog is letting you know that she's having a really exciting time.** If, however, your dog is looking a little too still, her mouth is closed and her ears are pulled back, then it's time to break up the party in a relaxed but definite way.

Your dog is very good at telling you how she's feeling in any given situation once you learn to read the signals. Other dogs rarely, if ever, make a mistake where canine mood and feelings are concerned—some, like tactless people, may ignore the signals, but few fail to understand their meaning.

A HIGHLY EXCITED DOG may offer other indicators in his body language: ears, tail, and facial expression all give separate clues.

Why does my dog ... respond more positively to low-voiced commands?

Q My partner and I trained our dog between us, making sure that we remained consistent, so that he received the same signals and body language whoever was running the training session. But our dog responds much more immediately to my partner's voice. I think it's because his pitch is lower; he claims that he's got more natural authority! Which of us is right?

A CONSISTENT RESPONSE to requests is crucial in dogs working for obedience and agility competitions, but it's just as important in daily life.

A Probably you. Pitch is important when you're asking your dog to pay attention, and the tone you use matters. The words have no intrinsic meaning to the dog but the tone does. Experienced trainers always tell novices to give a command only once, but in a cheerful, confident manner, as though there were no question of it being ignored.

There could be a number of reasons that your dog doesn't pay as much attention to you as to your partner—ask yourself if you do any of the following: Sound tentative? Sound apologetic? Repeat your request several times on a rising note (which your dog might well take as a signal to play)? Ask him to do something without checking your own body language (see pages 60–61)? Then look at how your partner asks your dog to do something—does he use a low, steady tone that expects to be taken seriously? Does he reward your dog at the moment that the dog starts the behavior requested (if you're calling "come," for example, the moment for praise is the instant the dog's body begins to move toward you, not the moment he arrives in front of you and stops moving).

If you find it hard to get your dog's attention in the first place, try a noise that couldn't be mistaken for a play noise. Say "hey!" sharply, or make a sharp, low gasp. Your dog will turn to see why you're making the noise—and you'll have a nanosecond in which you have his attention. And then use that tiny window of time to let him know, in a calm, cheerful voice, what it is that you want him to do.

SPECIES WATCH

Although dogs are smart in picking up what's required, the ultimate winner in cooperative teamwork with humans is the dolphin. Researchers have found that not only can dolphins pick up desired behavior with incredible speed, they also seem to be able to anticipate with uncanny accuracy what the next move or request from a human will be, demonstrating a way of thought that can seem remarkably similar to our own.

Chapter three

You and your dog

Never mind about why your dog does things ... have you ever wondered what your dog thinks about what YOU do? The questions that follow establish some of the key differences between the ways you look at the world, and the ways in which we believe your dog experiences some of the same things that you experience—the big issues of death, fear, and loneliness, as well as a topic that's been well proven to be important both to humans and to canines—social standing and the pecking order within our immediate packs. **Although we may not be able to say for sure how dogs see some of the things we do, their behavior can offer lots of clues**—and it's fascinating to try to read them.

Why does my dog … move away when I try to hug him?

Q My dog has no hesitation in approaching me for interaction and affection, but he doesn't like being hugged. Even if I just put my arm around him when we're sitting next to one another, he jumps up and moves away. I don't understand why a hug would worry him when he happily rolls over to have a belly rub (he often even initiates one by rolling over onto my feet when I'm doing something else). Surely he's far more vulnerable when he's lying on his back than sitting upright next to me with my arm around his shoulders?

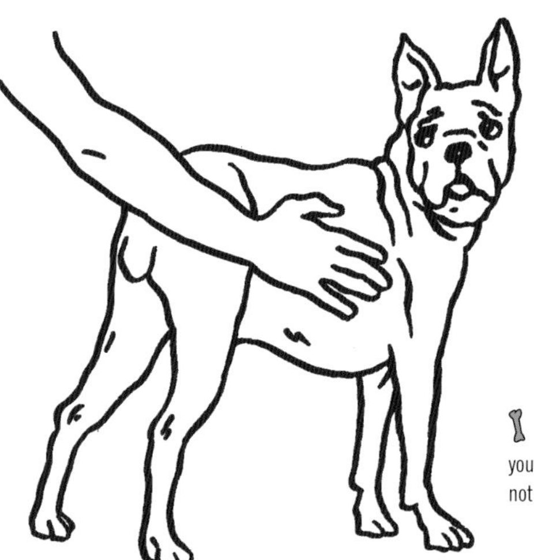

YOU'RE JUST EXPRESSING your affection—but that's not how your dog sees it.

A This is a classic example of a homonid misunderstanding. If you hugged a gorilla, he might be surprised by the inter-species contact, but he'd understand what the hug was intended to signify. Monkeys habitually hug one another, lay arms across one another's shoulders, and indulge in mutual grooming. But dogs have no such natural pattern. **To your dog your gesture resembles a "laying on of paws," which is typically a power move between dogs jockeying for position.** You may see it between dogs in boisterous play (one dog will put a paw insistently on the other's shoulder, raising him to a level higher than his playmate) or, more aggressively, between dogs who are fighting. But when you and your dog are sitting quietly together, a sudden arm around his shoulders, however affectionately intended, is puzzling and disquieting.

Many dogs will put up with a human cuddle when they know the human well, but even if they are used to accepting hugs, they will often try to convert the gesture into something more familiar to them—for example, by turning and covering the hugger's face with puppy licks, a gesture used by young dogs to demonstrate their supportiveness or perhaps an appeal to an older, senior dog. If you look carefully at the face of a dog accepting his owner's hug, his face is rarely quite as happy as that of his human.

As for the near-universal acceptance of a belly rub: your dog is inviting you to pet him. He knows you're not a threat to him, and the way he can show you this, and get a comforting massage into the bargain, is to roll over—a gesture to which he knows you're trained to respond.

SPECIES WATCH

Just as a pet dog may not recognize a hug, so we may misinterpret "human" forms of behavior in other species. Otters, for example, indulge in rafting, in which they float on their backs, apparently "holding paws." Behaviorists believe they do this for survival reasons: they can sleep while floating on the surface of the water while keeping their group together—literally "staying in touch."

IT'S ONLY PLAY but there's a serious underlying message.

Why does my dog ... appear not to care about the passing of her companion?

Q For the last five years we've had two dogs, both female labrador retrievers. They played together and seemed inseparable. But last month our older dog passed away at the age of 11. Not only were we upset to lose her, but we were also bracing ourselves to deal with a heartbroken younger dog. Far from it, our remaining pet has been behaving exactly as usual, cheerful and active, with a good appetite. Don't dogs understand death? Why doesn't she seem to mind the loss of her friend?

DOGS' REACTIONS to death vary hugely. Some seem to feel almost as humans do; others take the opportunity to remind us that they really are a different species.

A This is a question to which there really isn't a definite answer, although it's a very interesting one. There are numerous accounts of how dogs have reacted to the death of a companion with whom they've been apparently close, and reports are varied. Some dogs react in what their humans regard as a human way: stressed, sad, refusing to eat or play. To the human eye, they seem to be grieving. Others behave as you describe, remaining calm, energetic, and cheerful. A few even take on a new lease of life when their companions die which, behaviorists have suggested, is because the surviving dog gets more of what she wants without any canine competition, and that she appreciates it.

Some of us feel so close to our dogs that it's surprising when they don't react as a person would, forcibly reminding us that they are, after all, a different species.

Dogs are truthful in a way that humans aren't; one of the things that every owner knows is that a dog can't pretend to a feeling it doesn't have. So it may be that your dog, living in the moment as she does, finds life good now and doesn't think back or forward in the way that a person would.

If one takes this view, then the fact that some dogs seem to grieve becomes more surprising than that some dogs don't. However, many dogs are very sensitive to atmosphere, so their apparent grief may arise from an unease at the human unhappiness around them.

MOST DOGS appear to live in the present more than humans do. We can't know whether they're aware that they will never see their late companion again, or whether they're experiencing life "just for today."

Why does my dog... turn away and sniff the ground when other dogs approach?

Q My rescue dog is friendly, but not terribly confident in the company of others. He will play, but only after the other dog has made it clear that it's happy to engage; he never makes the first move himself. When he sees another dog in the distance, he'll watch it intensely until it comes quite close, then, just before it would seem natural to make eye contact, my dog will turn aside and sniff the ground, almost ostentatiously. Also, during play he licks his nose a lot; I've noticed this because he doesn't do it at any other time. Are these just his own idiosyncrasies, or is there something else going on?

NEGOTIATING SIGNALS are not unfriendly, but showing a sensible degree of caution.

A He may be shy, but his body language is fluent. Both the ground-sniffing and the nose-licking (behaviorists call this a tongue flick—it's just a very quick flick of the tongue over the nose and then back again, rather than prolonged licking) are negotiation signals to the approaching dog. They're part of a quite large repertoire of signs (see pages 10–11 for some of the others) that were originally christened "calming signals" by Turid Rugaas, an eminent Norwegian trainer who was one of the first to notice the clear patterns in the ways dogs signaled their good intent.

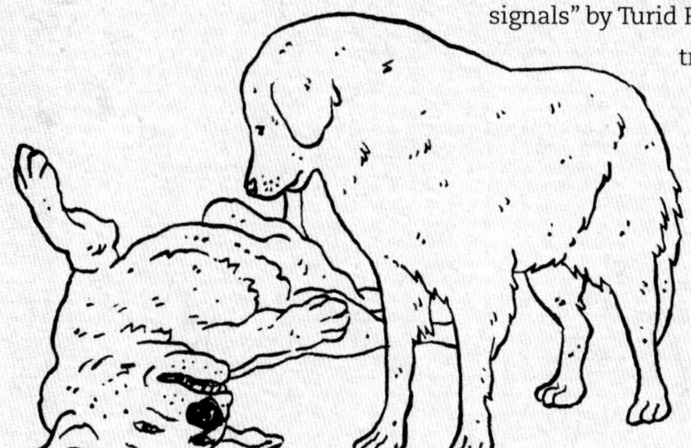

"I'M NOT A THREAT" Dogs who prostrate themselves and roll right over at the approach of another are usually very young or very timid: they're sending a signal that cannot be misread.

Rather than racing up and engaging with a dog he doesn't know, as a more confident animal might do, your pet is choosing to stand back and, by sniffing the ground, indicate that he's not aggressive or threatening in any way. Both animals know that they've spotted one another; your dog is leaving the forward part of the introduction to the approaching dog.

The tongue flick tends to be used a lot during play, and may be read as an acknowledgment to the other dog while your own is deciding on a course of action: perhaps a change of direction in the chase, or warning of a feint. It's widely used by dogs in general, although if a dog is licking his lips all the time (as opposed to just the quick flick of the tongue described above), it's an indicator, like constant yawning, that he's feeling nervous and a little stressed.

Why does my dog… not seem to be aware of her size?

Q I have a tiny chihuahua who is a lively and entertaining companion, but I find her almost worryingly feisty. She will march up to much, much larger dogs and introduce herself uncompromisingly, and she never seems to take any account of how tiny she is when she's playing, or when dogs are just milling around in a group. Other dogs seem to take her confidence in good part, but why doesn't she have more awareness of how tiny she is?

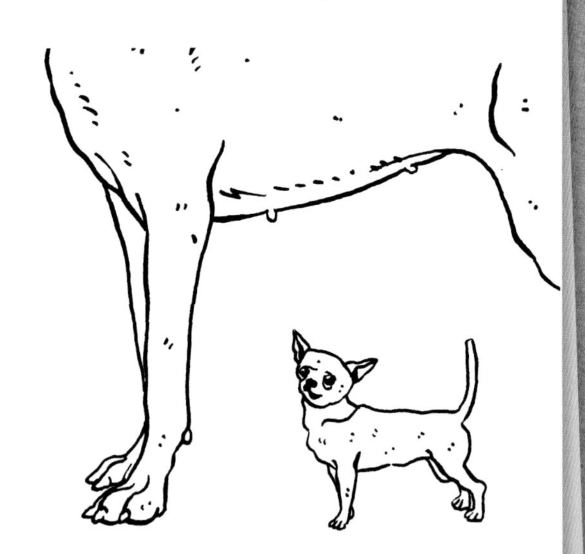

YOU'RE AS LARGE AS you feel and this tiny dog has all the confidence of others ten times her size.

A You have an alpha dog, and her consciousness of her high status makes her confident, regardless of the situation in which she finds herself. You know she's tiny, and that an aggressive larger dog could hurt her, but she's not expecting any challenges because she knows how high-ranking she is.

There would be more reason to worry if you had a dog who was an alpha-wannabe—the name many trainers use for dogs who are uncertain of their status in the pecking order, and keep trying to assert themselves. This mid-status level is responsible for many more problems than the self-appointed rank your chihuahua has awarded herself; **a dog who confidently expects others to defer to her will usually succeed in making them think that they should, too.** It's far from unknown for toy breeds to have this high sense of self-esteem, and you may be reinforcing it at home by indulging her self-importance in a way that you wouldn't with a larger dog.

The only problems that could arise with your little dog's sociable confidence is if she meets a genuinely aggressive dog and doesn't back down, or if another dog doesn't recognize her as a dog at all and sees her as prey. Make sure that however confident she may be, she also obeys you—a fast recall should get you out of any potentially difficult situations.

SPECIES WATCH

Size isn't everything; more than 65 million years ago, tiny shrewlike creatures existed alongside the dinosaurs that were then the major life forms on earth. The little mammals had comparatively large brains (compared to those of the dinosaurs, that is!) and were surprisingly similar to species of shrew that still exist today, long after the extinction of all dinosaur life.

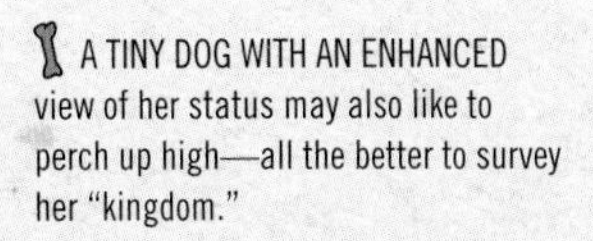

A TINY DOG WITH AN ENHANCED view of her status may also like to perch up high—all the better to survey her "kingdom."

Why does my dog … rush forward and try to lick my face when he's scolded?

Q Our spaniel is very well-attuned to human moods and seems extremely sensitive to changes in the tone and pitch of our family's voices. If he's scolded, he rushes forward and tries to reach my face; if I'm sitting and he can manage it, he'll clamber onto my knee and start licking my cheek. He looks as though he's in a paroxysm of anxiety, and he only calms down if I accept a thorough wash and talk to him soothingly. Why does he do this? Is he really upset?

IN HUMAN TERMS he might seem to be kissing you, but from a canine point of view, he's trying to appease you.

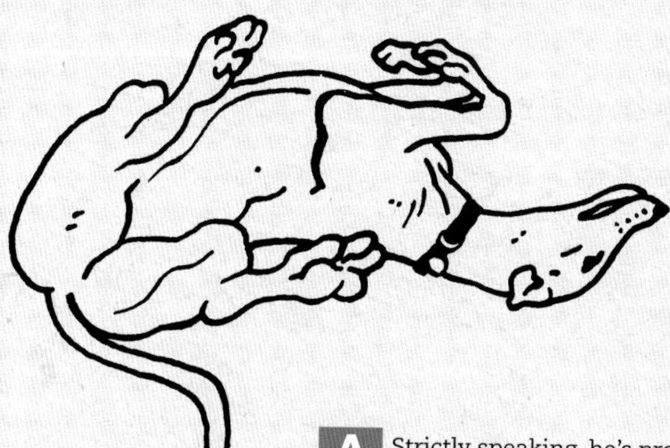

UPSIDE-DOWN Turning over onto the back, with belly exposed, is the most vulnerable position a dog can take up.

A Strictly speaking, he's probably not upset in the human sense; he's reacting entirely instinctively to your disapproval. In wolf and wild dog packs, the mothers wean their pups by regurgitating partially digested food for them; when the puppies lick and butt at the sides of their mother's faces, it's a request for food, and a reminder of their puppy status—small, helpless, needing to be looked after. And you can see the same thing in adult dogs. **If one dog wants to appease another, in particular one of a higher status, he will vigorously lick the side of his face in the same way, sending a similar signal: extend tolerance to me, I'm not a threat, look, I'm behaving like a puppy.**

This behavior is hardwired into dogs and has persisted long after they stopped regurgitating food for their pups. It's governed by the same impulse that will lead a worried dog to roll over in front of someone who's displeased with him, exposing his belly—another sign that the dog poses no threat. As with all polite dog approaches, you'll probably notice that your dog will move up to your face from the side, rather than face-to-face, which would be rudely direct in canine terms.

Why does my dog... bark when she hears other dogs barking?

Q Our family dog generally isn't noisy; she's lively and alert, but she tends not to express herself vocally. Recently a dog that barks a lot moved in a few doors away from us. He doesn't bark constantly, but he seems to have barking times, usually for brief periods in the evening, and our dog has begun to bark back. At other times, she barks no more than she ever did, but when the other dog is having a sustained barking bout, she'll start, too. She will sometimes even put her nose in the air and utter a noise that's almost a howl. It can be hard to quiet her down. Could she be answering the other dog? And is this a vestige of pack behavior?

REACHING BACK down the generations: howling is one of the most primitive sounds you'll ever hear from a contemporary domestic dog.

A She is answering the other dog. The bouts of barking you describe are typical of a dog that's been left alone and, in the absence of other members of his pack, wants to make contact with the outside world and to remind everyone that he's still there. Your dog is responding and letting the other dog know that she's there and can hear him.

Wolves and wild dogs aren't necessarily any more vocal than domestic dogs, but their barking patterns originally contained messages important for the safety of the pack—sounding an urgent alarm; letting other pack members know about incipient danger; making them aware of an individual's presence at a distance; and so on.

The most common reasons for a domestic dog's barking are loneliness (his pack or family have left him alone, and he wants to know if there's anyone around) and excitement (in play, or sometimes in frustration if a dog is longing to join in something but is prevented). The howl-like noise you describe your dog making is interesting; anyone who watches old Westerns will be aware that wolves generally use howling more than dogs do. In a wolf pack, a howl may be used by an individual to gather the pack together; although this is only speculation, it may be that your dog, aware of another dog not far away who is not a member of her own family, is seeking to gather her own pack around her and is making a noise to signal this.

SPECIES WATCH

All domesticated animals have a range of sounds, but the pig is probably the most expressive with more than 20 sounds, each of which seems to have a distinct and separate meaning. Sea mammals—whales, dolphins, and porpoises—are the gold medallists of sound in the animal world; sight and smell are of relatively little use deep under the sea, so their echolocation and noise-making skills have developed accordingly.

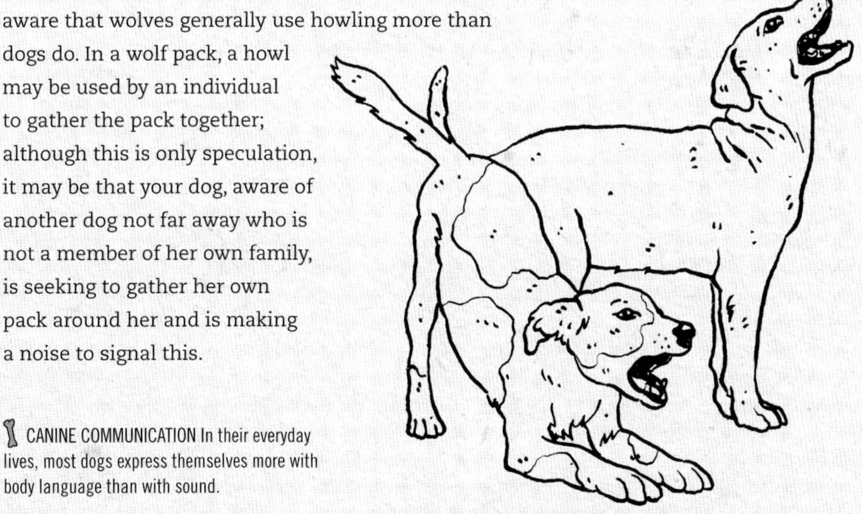

CANINE COMMUNICATION In their everyday lives, most dogs express themselves more with body language than with sound.

Why does my dog ... bark at bicycles and growl at men in hats?

Q We've had our dog for nearly a year; we first got him at six months old, and we don't know much about his early puppyhood. He's easygoing, mixed breed, and medium sized; he generally gets along well with people and other dogs and is very tolerant with our children. But he goes into a frenzy over just two things: he can't see a bicycle without going into a barking fit, and he seems both excited by and mistrustful of men wearing hats. Otherwise he's not particularly excitable. Why does he hate these two things—and how can we teach him to calm down around them?

IT'S YOUR DOG'S prerogative to decide what worries him, and it's your job to sort it out.

A If you weren't involved in the early socialization of your dog, you may never know what caused the original wariness of hats and bikes. **Experts have established that the key period in which dogs absorb new experiences and develop strategies for coping with the unexpected comes between eight and 12 weeks;** dogs that have negative or very limited experiences of the human world over this time may find it harder to deal with new things later. Although you don't know whether your dog was frightened by a man in a hat, you may be able to overcome his concern by gently introducing hats in a situation where he doesn't feel threatened.

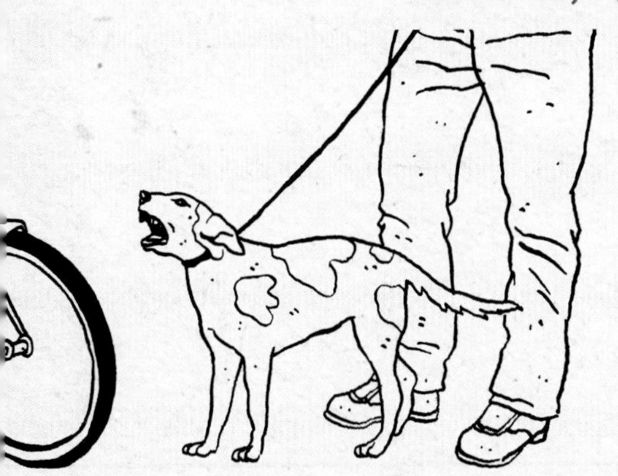

FRIGHT OR FLIGHT? Does your dog fear the bicycle, or does he really want to chase it?

Enlist some male friends your dog already knows and is comfortable with to sit and give him treats for a while, hat alongside, and, by stages, link treats and hat—the treats might go in the hat, the hat might be held by the hand that's giving the treats, and so on. Always go very gently: the fear may seem foolish to you, but it's your dog's right to decide what frightens him, just as it's your job to try to overcome it.

Barking at bicycles (if they're moving) may not be the result of fear: your dog's chasing impulse may be coming into play. Barking at a moving bike through a window, could be the result of frustration; your dog wants to chase the bike, but can't get at it. It goes without saying that he can't be allowed to chase bikes, so try distraction techniques to break the pattern and make sure that he's leashed in areas where there are likely to be bicycles when he's out of doors.

Why does my dog … act like he doesn't hear me when he's off chasing squirrels?

Q My dog was easy to train and he's very responsive and obedient, with just one exception. In open areas, when he's off the leash, if he sees a squirrel, he's gone. And, worse, he just doesn't seem to hear me at all when I call him back to me. I'd understand this if he was usually willful, but he isn't; he's generally a great companion who's also extremely reliable. So why does he completely ignore me in the thrill of the chase?

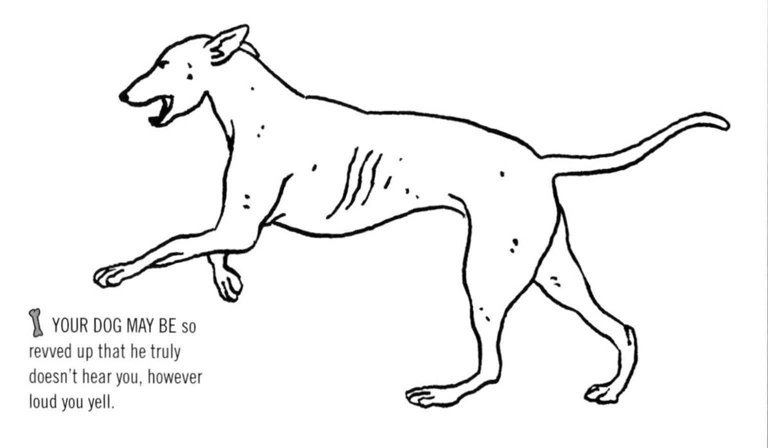

YOUR DOG MAY BE so revved up that he truly doesn't hear you, however loud you yell.

A You probably will never cure your dog of his temporary deafness in situations as extreme as this; if he can't hear you, he can't pay attention to what you're saying. If you're somewhere where it matters that he shouldn't chase (that is, anywhere but safe, open countryside without any farm animals around), you should keep him leashed; when he's off the leash in an area where it won't be the end of the world if he does take off, make a habit of calling him back to you every few minutes anyway—use the recall just to remind him that you're there. **If he's in the habit of coming back when he's not highly excited, you stand a better chance of catching his attention when he's in the process of responding to something exciting**—before he reaches the point at which instinct has taken over completely and he's deaf and blind to anything but the chase.

SPECIES WATCH

Dogs aren't the only species that can go deaf with excitement; studies on domestic cats showed the same process when they were subjected to an extremely strong stimulus—it blotted out all consciousness of even loud sounds. Quantities of adrenaline in the system can heighten some senses and suppress others. The "fight or flight" chemical reaction in the brain is well named.

AT THE CALM STAGE, a dog can be very engaged and interested (what's that chicken doing?), but still be able to turn his attention to you—he hasn't yet gone deaf with arousal.

Why does my dog… get confused when I change the way I say commands?

Q Our dog is smart, but she seems to get confused sometimes when I'm asking her to do something. My question relates to how important the words are when you're teaching obedience. She responds to a whole range of variations on "come" such as "come here," "here girl," and "here Rosie;" however, she seems to confuse "sit" and "stay." How can she seem to understand some requests in a range of forms, while she mixes up other simple ones?

DOGS DON'T SPEAK ENGLISH, so you should ensure that you give them all the help you can when you're asking them to do something.

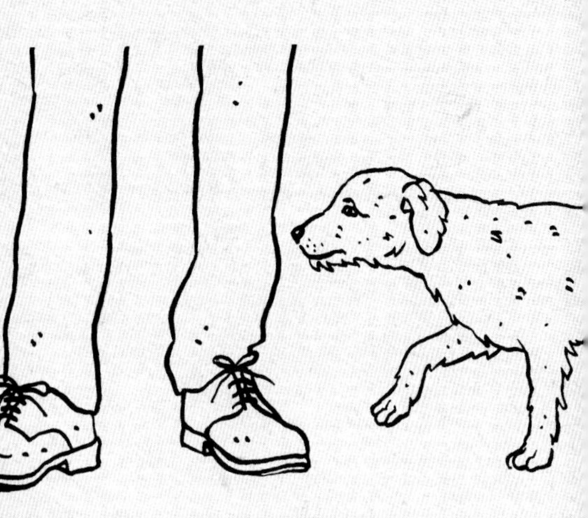

SOMETIMES A COMMUNICATION PROBLEM is being caused by human muddle rather than canine confusion.

A Your dog doesn't understand your confusing directions because she doesn't speak English. When she's figuring out what you're asking, she responds to a whole range of signals you send: the pitch of your voice, your tone, and your body language. Consistency in all of these is crucial. **Dogs reported as "stubborn" in training are almost always confused—they don't understand what it is that their human wants from them, so they don't do anything.** "Come" is usually easy for dogs to learn; rewarded by treats and praise, it generally proves to be the no-brainer in the training manual. Rosie is likely to be responding to signals that you're sending with your body as well as with your voice when you call her to you, and won't be paying too much attention to the various sounds you're making. "Sit" and "stay" may be harder for her to distinguish because you're keeping your body still for these commands and sending her fewer clues.

The real question, though, is why ask your dog to play guessing games? However smart she is (and she's smart enough to try to read the various signals you send her, and usually get the answer right), it's simpler and ultimately kinder to give her clear, unequivocal requests. Find one way of asking her to do each thing (you may need to go back to the beginning) and stick to it. Don't give her needless complications when she's learning. You need to get the basics right with your smart dog, and you need to be smart enough yourself to teach her in a way that's easy for her to grasp and retain.

Why does my dog ... not want to play?

Q Our rescue dog came to us six months ago, at the age of four. He had a horribly abusive background, and we had to start from the beginning and take everything gently and slowly with him. He's progressed in leaps and bounds: his coat is now glossy, he's eating well, he is clean around the house, and he's become much less timid on his walks. He even seems to enjoy contact with gentle, older dogs, although he's still scared of anyone—person or dog—who's too exuberant and bouncy. But he doesn't seem to know how to play—we've tried sticks, balls, and squeaky toys, but none seems to spark his interest. He just looks rather sadly at them and turns away. We find this heartbreaking; can we teach him to play, or is it too late?

A RESCUE DOG who has been concentrating purely on survival won't have had space for play in his past.

A It's not necessarily too late. Your dog may never enjoy energetic play and he may remain too nervous to play in a group, but there are some things you can do that may engage him. If food is a strong motivator for him (and it's often particularly important to dogs who have suffered hunger in the past), stuff a Kong toy with something he'll enjoy—you can buy liver- or other flavored pastes just for this, or if you have a run of hot weather you could experiment with the frozen gravy treat described on page 29. Your pet will at first enjoy the food for its own sake, but may come to enjoy investigating the Kong toy for the positive associations the food gives it. As a second step, you could buy one of those playballs that conceal treats—rather than sitting working the food out of the toy, the dog is required to play a slightly more active role, rolling it around until the treats fall out. Again, it's a step toward having your dog roll around the ball because he enjoys it, and it may guide him toward investigating other toys for the experiences they offer.

Dogs who have been seriously deprived since they were tiny puppies often have had to concentrate so hard on the basics of survival that they missed many of the growing up and development stages that come naturally to pups from happier backgrounds. Your dog isn't even a teenager any more—he's passed his life up to young adulthood in deprived circumstances, so it's not surprising that playing isn't high on his agenda. Continue to provide the gentle, consistent support he needs and to experiment with new interests for him and, if you give him a little more time, you may be pleasantly surprised.

IF TOYS CONNECT with something a deprived dog already values, such as food, they're more likely to engage his attention.

SPECIES WATCH

Species that naturally play constantly when young seem to suffer more than others when socially deprived. In research, rats, who are highly social and play for prolonged periods when young, displayed much more stress than guinea pigs, gerbils and mice, none of which have the same playful pattern as part of their growing up process, and which have a much lower response to the absence of interaction.

Why does my dog… get so possessive about the sofa?

Q We have two couches and a couple of armchairs in our living room, and there's plenty of room for everyone to sit comfortably—including our year-old mastiff, who is allowed on the furniture. But recently she's begun to grumble at me when I sit down alongside her. She's a big dog, but so far she's been amenable to train and easy to manage. The first time she did it, I pushed her out of the way and sat where she'd been sitting. The second time, her grumble went up a notch or two (although not as far as a growl), and I felt a little intimidated, so I left her there. How can I nip this behavior in the bud without turning it into a drama?

POSSESSION may be nine-tenths of the law, but you don't want it to apply to your sofa.

A You're right to be concerned; with a large, powerful dog like this, you need to be confident that she will do as you say. At a year old your pet is still a teenager, and she is experimenting with her ranking within the household. The difficulty here is that you need to clarify who's in charge (you), without ever turning a situation into a confrontation. As soon as your dog is challenged to the point where she feels she needs to growl, you've lost the game (and, should it ever happen, you should seek professional advice). **Your dog has looked at her position in your surroundings and has decided that she is, or could be, top dog.** So get rid of this assumption, which should solve the sofa problem.

Tighten up the rules for your pet; you mention that she's been amenable to train and manage, so institute a firmer regime. Her treats must be privileges that she needs to earn. Work with what she knows already; if she brings her ball for a game, get her to sit down before you throw it. Ask her to sit and stay before meals, and don't put her food bowl down on the floor until she does.

Since the sofa seems to have become an important area to her, start offering her a treat to get off it, and put her into a "sit" before you give it to her. If anyone else in the household plays with her or gives her meals, make sure that they know the rules and ensure that they're applied consistently. Keep things cheerful; you need to be firm, not heavy handed. The message your dog will get is that, after all, she doesn't take precedence over you, and that her meals and fun are within your power to grant—or withhold. As the message sinks in, she will naturally begin to look to you for guidance, and the inappropriate "resource guarding" of the sofa should stop.

MAKE IT CLEAR that food and fun are within your power to give, and your dog's respect for you should grow.

Why does my dog… need to perceive me as her pack leader?

Q When we got our Newfoundland dog, who's now two years old, I bought masses of behavior and training manuals—we'd chosen such a big breed that I wanted to be certain that I was on top of her training and understood how she behaved. She's a wonderful dog with a calm nature and her behavior has never given us a moment's worry. Yet most of the books I've bought stress over and over again that it's important that your pet regards you as their "pack leader," and the advice is strict—some even recommend that I make my dog roll over on her back to show that she's subservient and obedient to me. Do I really need to be forceful with her to make her understand that I'm the boss?

JUST BECAUSE A DOG is large it doesn't mean that she'll think she rules the roost; some dogs really are gentle giants.

A PACK LEADER should command respect whatever the breed or size of their canine charges.

A whole book could be written in answer to this question, but here's the short version. Up until the last few years, it was widely believed that dogs responded best to forceful training with constant reminders that their human owners were "boss" in any situation. Under this system, it was thought that people should dominate their dogs in order to provide the sort of strong leadership believed to prevail in wild dog and wolf packs. However, this argument has been largely discredited by research into animals in the wild and greater knowledge of the behavior of dogs in domestic situations. **Increasingly, a style of unnecessarily dominant management of dogs at home is seen as creating more behavioral problems than it solves, by making animals confused—and worse, fearful—as they fail to understand what their owners are asking of them.** It sounds as though you've been reading some books that still adhere to this thinking.

"If it works, don't fix it." Your Newfoundland isn't giving you any problems and has accepted you as leader quite happily, so carry on as you are. She may simply not be very status-conscious—some dogs aren't, and they're often the ones who are easiest to live with. On the question of strict treatment, most modern behaviorists don't believe in governing your pets by force; rather, they try to get to the root of any problems and look at ways the owners can dispel problematic patterns for the dog by sending signals that the dog will understand, and that will work against the unwanted behavior.

SPECIES WATCH

How to placate an angry individual who outranks you is a problem solved in different ways by different species. Male savanna baboons, widely found in Africa, will get a hold of a baboon baby and hold it up if approached aggressively by a senior male—the presence of the baby apparently inhibits the other male's impulse to attack and settles the situation safely all round.

Chapter four

Solving problems

Maybe your dog is possessive with his toys, maybe he's not responsive to training, or maybe he's suffering from separation anxiety. Dog owning has its share of worries as well as pleasures, and the following pages look at a few of them, then give you several suggestions as to what your dog's train of thought may be, as well as some ideas for getting around some of the problem behavior. Thinking about dog behavior has changed over the last decade; **solving problems is now far less about punishing the dog and far more about trying to understand the dog's reasons for behaving in a certain way,** as well as introducing ways to replace the problem habit with something that the dog will enjoy and that is more acceptable to humans. Much more is understood about the ways in which dogs think than was known 20 years ago, although ultimately there will always be a certain amount about the canine mind that, separated by species, we can only make an informed guess at.

Why does my dog … ignore me when I shout at her?

Q Our dog is just emerging from teenagerhood—she's a lurcher with a good turn of speed and—apparently—a good sense of humor. But I have problems getting her to take me seriously; she doesn't seem to recognize when playtime stops and I'm asking for obedience. If we're in the park and we've been having a lively game but it's time to bring it to a close and I tell her so, she seems to go deaf. In fact, she'll gambol up to me as though I'd personally invited her to carry on playing a game with just me. If I try to put her on a leash, she'll dart away. If I shout at her, she seems to take it in her stride and play even harder. What am I doing wrong, and why won't she listen to me?

"I JUST CAN'T HEAR YOU!" Your dog's stance may not be naughty; she may be suffering from stimulus overload.

A Your dog isn't recognizing your signals. This isn't a question of a highly excited dog literally not hearing you (like the example on pages 88–89); she can hear you but she either doesn't read your tone of voice or—and this may be where the sense of humor comes in—is choosing not to read it. You mention that this happens when she's playing with you, rather than roughhousing with a group of other dogs, so she's already paying attention to you; she's just not hearing what you want her to hear. **Dogs apparently can't always distinguish between the import in voices that are high, excited, and fast.** You may be shouting, "Come, come, come," but to your dog's ear, the sound may be very similar to the noises that you were making when you were playing together in the exciting game of chase that she's trying to prolong.

To catch her attention, try using your usual command. If she recalls to "come," say the word just once, but lower your pitch considerably. Your dog's revved up and she doesn't want to stop, so it will be easier to catch her attention by doing something different. Some trainers recommend that you simply sit down, then call your dog; the unexpected body language may distract her from the game she's playing. It may also be easier to get her attention without having to shout if you wind an energetic chasing game down slowly, rather than switching from high activity to a request for obedience.

Slow down the chase, then use whichever signal you've chosen for recall, called once in a low but clear and carrying tone. When your dog can hear the difference in your voice, she's more likely to recognize the request you're making.

Reassurance signals are often exchanged between animals who live in social groups. The primate expert Frans de Waal found "making friends" behavior in chimpanzees, bonobos, and macaque monkeys, from mutual grooming to, in the case of chimpanzees, actually kissing, as a way of reassuring one another that things had gone back to normal after a fight.

Why does my top dog... come between others when trouble looms?

Q I have always owned dogs and at the moment we have four at home, two males and two females. The two young male dogs play together a lot, but also have a tendency to scrap; they've never come to serious blows, but they do squabble and snap a fair amount. My older female rules the roost overall, and tends to remain above any petty arguments between the other three, but now and then when the two males are jockeying for position, she'll get in between them and just stand, without doing anything, until she's separated them. Once they're apart, she'll calmly return to her seat on the sofa. What's happening, is it a problem, and should I interfere?

WITHOUT A SENIOR to take charge, a minor misunderstanding could lead to a full-blown quarrel.

A Absolutely not. You have a dog who is not only a confident leader but also a great negotiator between the other members of your pack, and there's no need for any human intervention. What you've observed has also been widely written about by dog behaviorists. **Your senior dog has spotted something more serious and worrying than just jockeying for seniority in the interaction between the other two—and it doesn't seem to her like part of a game.** So she's cooling the mood by literally getting in between the other two before it gets too intense or turns into a full-fledged fight. You only see this sort of negotiation when you have a senior dog who is calm, sensible, and takes her role seriously. This makes your job as overall pack leader much easier.

You may never be able to see what she understands in the body language between your two male dogs. It may be the miniscule movement of an ear; a very slight tension in a face or tail; or a tiny change in the stance of one of the protagonists. There's even been some suggestion among researchers that a key change in mood may be signaled to others by a change in the scent of the increasingly tense dog. While there's no conclusive evidence for this, given that a dog's sense of smell is so much stronger than a human's, as a theory it doesn't seem too far-fetched.

Whatever it is, your older female spots it before the situation explodes and acts calmly and without fuss to calm things down. And as soon as she has done the minimum necessary, and reminded everyone of their respective ranking, she goes back to what she was doing before the disturbance—in this case, ruling the roost from the sofa.

Why does my dog … constantly come to me for reassurance?

Q I live alone with my two-year-old mixed breed dog. She's a great companion and is generally sociable. However, she seems to lack confidence; in any situation that feels at all crowded or involves people she doesn't know, she will come to me apparently asking for reassurance. This may take the form of her butting my knee with her head, weaving between my ankles, or trying to get on a level so that she can lick my face. Why isn't she more confident, what's behind these displays, and is there any way that I can stop them?

TO HUMANS, it's natural to offer reassurance, but to dogs, it proves that there really is something to be nervous about.

A It sounds as though your dog missed out on some of the ideal socialization that's so important while puppies are still young. If she's badly thrown by the unfamiliar, there are things that you can do to help her become more comfortable, although you're unlikely ever to be able to turn a shy dog into a gung-ho, sociable one. What do you do when she comes to you and acts needy?

The obvious route taken by many owners who find themselves in a similar position is to pet their dogs, offering comfort and support. Although this is a very natural (human) way to behave, it won't help the dog gain confidence. Instead, consolation when the dog is feeling shy is likely to be counterproductive. You'll be sending her a double message: first, that there's something to be scared of (after all, you're acknowledging her concerns); and second, by giving her your attention and making a fuss of her, that you actually like her to behave in this fearful way.

Instead, look for any opportunities for positive reinforcement. Your dog went (nervously, but hopefully) to greet an unfamiliar visitor? Quick, have that visitor give her a treat. In fact, **arm visitors with treats at your front door, and ask that they scatter them around wherever they're sitting.** When she comes up to them and initiates contact herself, then they can pet her calmly.

Conversely, when your dog comes to you for comfort in an unfamiliar situation, ignore her. Don't reward her timidity with attention. This may feel a little strange or even mean at first, but as she learns that the unfamiliar may be the source of treats and praise, and that acting scared won't pay any dividends, she's more likely to chance braver behavior.

Why has my dog ... become so obsessive about her toys?

Q My two-year-old Jack Russell terrier has always enjoyed playing. She likes hard toys, ideally ones that squeak, and she will play with them tirelessly, growling, shaking them, and throwing them up in the air. She's extremely protective about them, however, and this, together with the intensity of her play, is beginning to worry us a little. Why is she so fierce with them, and how can we stop her guarding them like this?

MOST DOGS VALUE THEIR TOYS, but it makes sense to prevent your dog from becoming too obsessive about her beloved playthings.

A She's fierce with her toys because she's acting out her heritage: Jack Russell terriers were originally bred to deal with prey ranging from rats and rabbits to foxes, "going to ground"—that is, descending into their dens and burrows—after them when necessary and either flushing them out or finishing them off down there. The challenges that terriers pose owners when they're chosen as domestic pets can usually be traced back to their breeding background: tenacious, obstinate, and independent-minded, they need dedicated training to keep their energetic personalities in check.

What you see when your terrier takes hold of a toy, squeaks it repeatedly, then fiercely shakes it from side to side with all her force, is an enactment of the typical terrier kill. If she were hunting, she'd seize her prey by the nape and then give it a hard shake to break its neck. And the level of her excitement is the same as that she'd bring to the hunt.

Given how much enjoyment they bring her, it's hardly surprising that she guards her toys so firmly. The energy of her play is nothing to worry about—she's simply being a terrier—but if you want to calm down her propensity to guard a notch or two, get her used to the idea of exchanging one toy for another. Arm yourself with a handful of the squeaking toys she loves, then squeak one toy while she's playing with another. As she rushes to grab it from you, hand it over and pick up the first one. At first, she'll dash back to her first choice; hand it over to her immediately, then squeak a third toy and repeat the process. Always give her back the toy she's given up immediately when she looks for it. Make this a daily exercise: the lesson you're teaching her is that she can have her toy—and the other one, too.

Why does my dog... become so unhappy around children?

Q We have two dogs and three adults in our household—but no children. However, we have many friends with kids and they often visit. One of our dogs—a border collie—loves children and always engages with them; she has a tendency to herd them, but gently. Her daughter, however, seems to dread their visits; she'll hide away behind furniture or go in another room to avoid any contact with them, and is miserable as long as they are around. Why are the dogs so different, and why does the younger dog seem to feel so strongly about it?

TIME OUT may be the answer for a dog who is fearful of small children. Don't let young ones follow a shy dog around; she may feel cornered and turn defensive.

A There are many things about kids—especially young kids—which can be disturbing to dogs. Toddlers, in particular, may really frighten them. A small child doesn't respect personal space, is at face level to many dogs, and communicates in very high-pitched, unpredictable squeals and shouts, the latter particularly disturbing to sound-sensitive dogs. Kids also tend to stare unblinkingly at objects of interest, which dogs may read as a challenge, and may grab at the dog if it is within reach.

If you take all these factors into consideration, it's not so surprising that some dogs don't like kids; in fact, it becomes rather more surprising that any dogs do! Your two dogs represent the extremes: your older dog enjoys the lively herding opportunities that they offer, while your younger one probably dislikes them for some or all of the reasons listed here.

Opinions differ as to why certain dogs do tolerate children well. Some favor a breed explanation, and would say, for example, that herding breeds enjoy having something relatively small to gather and manage. This explanation doesn't explain the fear of your younger dog, however. It's also been mooted, although only speculatively, that dogs who have raised litters are more likely to recognize something about kids that marks them as young animals, and that an experienced dam will adopt an inclusive approach to young kids. Whatever the explanation, be tolerant of your younger dog's feelings and don't expose her to kids who are too young to understand that she must be respected. And, whatever you do, never leave any children in her vicinity without careful supervision of both children and dog.

Why does my dog... behave badly at the front door?

Q Our dog has always been rather barky and excitable at the front door, but recently he's become nearly unmanageable when someone calls. He'll barge in front of me, bark and jump up at visitors, and generally be a complete menace. Worse, although his excitement is mercifully good tempered, the noise levels and his pushiness mean that some of our less animal-friendly visitors are becoming frightened of him. Why does he do this, and how can we get him to behave like a civilized member of the household again when someone calls?

IT'S A NOISY JOB and, from your pet's point of view, it's also a crucial one: someone has to keep an eye on who's coming onto his territory.

A It may be cold comfort, but loud, rude behavior (rude from the human viewpoint, anyway) at the front door is one of the commonest discipline problems. **Most dogs have a healthy regard for the front door as the entry to home territory, and a place that everyone else in the family treats as important—after all, when the doorbell rings, you usually come running.** So your dog is actually responding to his perception of your arousal level: first of all he followed your lead, and now he's taking the initiative.

When you reach the door, you're loudly telling him to hush before you open it—again, from his point of view, you are "barking," so he deduces there's just cause for it and ramps up the noise a bit. Add in more rebukes as you tell him to back off, and his excitement rises to fever pitch: clearly what's going on at the front door is justification for any level of stimulation.

The good news is that with a bit of persistence, the vicious circle of excitement/barking, more excitement/more barking, can usually be broken. You need to practice with friends, so that at first you are in control of when a knock at the door is going to happen. The idea is to teach your dog that the knock is a trigger for him to get a treat in another room, so the technique is to offer your dog something delicious at the exact instant that a knock comes on the door.

Absolute consistency (and having a supply of treats at hand in case of an unexpected knock) usually pays off, in that a dog will come to see the knock as the signal for a piece of liver—off-site. When he's had his treat in the appointed place—and it should always be the same one—lead him to the front door and ask him to sit before you answer it, maintaining control of the situation and relieving your pet of the idea that he must play sentry.

SPECIES WATCH

Territorial guarding is widespread across the whole animal kingdom. Methods of guarding vary from the elegant to the actively aggressive. Sometimes elaborate displays take the place of any actual contact, from the fearsome chest beating of the gorilla to the puffed-up, vivid pink dewlap of the small green anole lizard. Many species seem to be aware, consciously or otherwise, of the power of bluff.

Why does my dog … suddenly insist on sitting up so high?

Q I have a smart, small, mixed-breed dog. She's five years old and we've never had any concerns about her until recently; she's easygoing with the family and has always appeared friendly to our baby, who has just turned one. Recently, though, she seems to have become obsessed with sitting on the furniture. Not a problem in itself, but if anyone else sits down, she'll try to climb higher than them—onto the arm, or even the back of the chair. Is this a status thing, or a sign of something else?

SITTING IN COMFORT, but is your dog also looking for an advance in status?

A This is a complicated one, and it's hard to be certain without seeing her in action, but it probably does have something to do with her perception of her status. Your mention of your baby, who is probably quite mobile, made us wonder if that was an element in the puzzle, too. As you'll have gathered from questions in earlier chapters, some dogs are acutely aware of their place in the scheme of things and take any change in the status quo as a cue to advance themselves within their family structure, while others remain laid back.

Your dog may be trying to raise her status literally—by climbing higher and higher as others join her on a chair or sofa—or she may be expressing something more complicated. If your baby has just turned into a toddler, he may threaten your pet's comfort in her surroundings and this odd climbing behavior may be a mixed signal: she could be staying out of the way, while trying to ensure that her place in the family isn't threatened.

As usual with an animal who is acting in a conflicted way, tighten up the rules around her for a while. Most dogs are reassured by things going on as normal. If the baby's seated on a lap, make sure your dog is asked to stay on the floor (you could put her through a short sit and stay routine, and reward her for complying), and make sure that you never, ever leave your baby and your dog alone together.

Older children can be taught to be respectful of dogs, but toddlers are too small to understand that the canine members of the family shouldn't be grabbed at. Also, they're at the face-to-face level that is most disconcerting for the dog. Be vigilant, give your dog regular attention and training exercises, and you may find that the sofa-climbing behavior diminishes.

Why does my dog ... try to mount visitors?

Q My adolescent terrier has become much more assertive in his behavior and difficult to manage since he hit the eight-month point. We were warned at his puppy training class that dogs have a teenage stage, and were ready with extra exercise, a daily training session, and plenty of things to occupy him. What we weren't prepared for, however, were his assaults on visitors' legs—comical sometimes, but also embarrassing on occasion. He must know they're not female dogs, so why does he try to mount human shins?

TO YOU, it looks like a human leg; to your adolescent dog, it's an opportunity to reinforce his status in the world.

A Just as your breeder warned, he's a teenager and his hormones are running high. Despite appearances, however, this sort of mounting isn't sexual behavior—even your hormone-crazed pet knows the difference between a receptive female and a human leg—in fact, it's not even exclusively male behavior, it's sometimes seen in female dogs, too. It's power-humping: he's trying to impress those around him with his rank and status. As you say, it can be embarrassing, and with some dogs it seems to become obsessive: they'll mount not just human legs but even soft toys and pillows—in fact, anything they can get a firm grip on.

Getting on top of things—literally climbing for rank—is natural in dogs. Even as tiny puppies, young dogs will wrestle and climb on top of each other and in older dogs the "laying on of paws," in which a dog raises himself by laying a paw over another's back, is very commonly seen both in play and in real fighting. If you want to put a stop to this jockeying for position, you'll probably find it most effective to create a diversion rather than simply rebuking your dog. Say "Hey!" sharply, then, as soon as you've got your dog's attention, offer a toy, or put him through a short routine (this can be as simple as "sit, stay" and treat—anything to distract him from his own humping preoccupation!).

The best way to get through the canine teenage stage is with plenty of positive reinforcement for the behavior you do want, and quick, sharp distractions from the behavior you don't—that way, you're ensuring that your dog will remain keen to interact with you, because you make things interesting and fun, rather than simply stopping him from doing what he wants.

Why does my dog… get so anxious when I leave the house?

Q My pet—a four-year-old hound cross—has never enjoyed being left alone and has had a tendency to whine and make a fuss when I leave the house, but over the last year her anxiety seems to have become unmanageable for her. I often come home to find that she's destroyed something—chewed a cushion or a shoe to pieces, for example. I get an almost hysterical welcome when I come in. She doesn't have to be left a lot, because I work at home, so my absences tend to be for two or three hours in the evening. Can I make things easier for her, and why has this anxiety arisen?

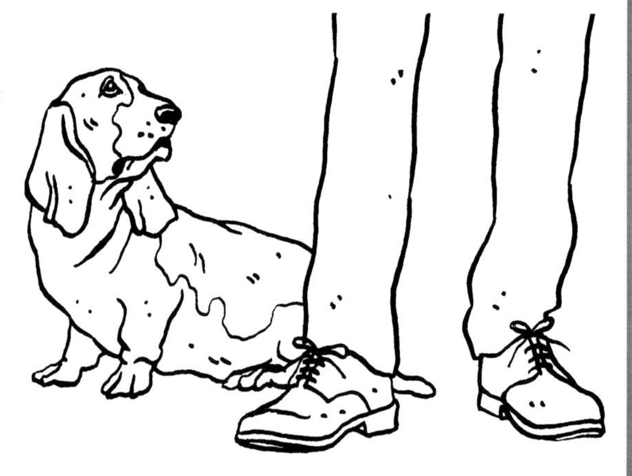

NO DOG LIKES being left alone, but to some, being without you causes unbearable anxiety.

A Separation anxiety is common and there is a range of theories as to its underlying cause. Some behaviorists believe that it's a sign that a dog aspires to be leader in your pack, and finds the fact that she has no control over your movements when you go out difficult—the rationale goes that the dog becomes anxious because she doesn't even know where her human is, much less being able to manage him or her. Others think it is just that a dog finds it lonely and boring to be without any company. How easy it is to ease a pet's anxiety depends on her personality. There are various things that you can try, although this is a problem that sometimes calls for professional help.

First, **don't reinforce the anxiety by making reassuring noises to your dog before you go out, and making a fuss over her when you come back in.** This is more likely to strengthen her conviction that there's something to worry about when you go out. Whenever you go out, go calmly. Leave your dog with something interesting to do (if she calms down a little she'll prefer to be kept busy by trying to get some liver out of a toy, for example, than by tearing up a cushion). When you return, greet your dog quietly and ignore any hysterical displays. If possible, redirect her to some obedience exercises, which encourage her to concentrate.

Some trainers suggest that the owners of anxious dogs defuse their expectations by varying the routine of going out. In this technique, you go out for a minute only, then come back in again. Or you put your coat on, but then don't go out. The thinking behind this is that your dog gets confused about whether you're going out or not; deprived of the triggers for her anxiety (you're breaking the rules, or mixing them up), she cannot keep it at a peak, so starts to let go of it.

SPECIES WATCH

Anxiety isn't limited to mammals, or even to comparatively complex animals; research into very simple organisms have shown that they can suffer, too. In one study, sea snails learned to anticipate tiny regular shocks and experienced a chemical reaction in anticipation of them; they were calmed only after a lengthy period during which they were allowed to graze on seaweed undisturbed.

Why does my dog… fail to respond to my commands?

Q I've owned and trained literally dozens of dogs and have had good relationships with all my pets. About six months ago, I was asked to take on a bulldog/terrier mix, whose owner had died, and as I'd recently lost my own dog, I agreed. He is ten months old, and has me baffled. I know that he's not stupid, and he has an agreeable personality, but I can't seem to get him through the simple training exercises that have worked with my other dogs. What is his problem?

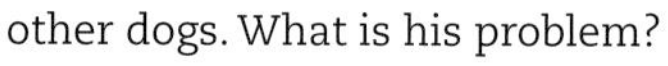

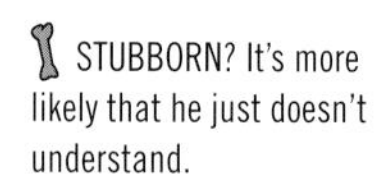

STUBBORN? It's more likely that he just doesn't understand.

A His problem is that he's a different dog with different needs from the other dogs you've owned and trained. **All dogs are individuals, and what works even for 99 percent of the canine population may not work for the one who's more individual than most.** We're assuming that your pup hasn't come from an abusive background, in which case, you would need some special help. Otherwise, it seems he just has a slightly different or more independent personality than your other dogs. While consistency, patience, and an enjoyable training schedule work for the vast majority of dogs, the nature of the schedule may need to change according to the dog. And, of course, dogs haven't read the rule books—your new recruit only knows that, at the moment, your tried-and-trusted methods aren't working for him.

Working with a dog who doesn't immediately get your training is useful to you because it encourages you to try some imaginative training ideas other than the ones you're used to. Buy and read some new training manuals, study your dog, and, most important, discover what he values most: Face time with you? A specific toy or food? A favorite game? When you've found what it is, use it as an incentive. You might want to experiment with clicker training if you haven't tried it up to now—it works well with a lot of dogs because the absolute consistency of the clicking noise gets their attention easily and, once they've associated it with rewards, they automatically concentrate more closely on their trainer.

Whatever you do, don't give up—it's especially rewarding when you find a training pattern that works with a challenging dog. And keep sessions short and upbeat to ensure that your dog enjoys working with you.

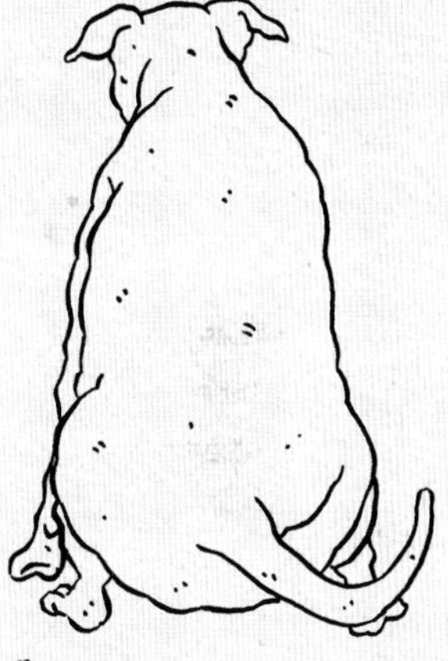

DON'T PERSIST if one sort of training doesn't seem to be working; try to engage your dog in different ways.

Why does my dog… need me to dominate?

Q Our neighbor has a three-year-old boxer who he trains extremely regularly and, it seems to me, harshly, although he stops short of physical correction. We have just acquired a boxer puppy to replace our previous dog, who died last year. I've trained our last two dogs myself and have not had any problems, although it has to be said that neither were ever quite as obedient as our neighbor's dog. He insists that you have to "show a dog who's master," and that unless you dominate your dog you can't rely on its behavior. I would not want to be as tough as he is in training. Which of us is right, and is it really necessary for me to dominate my dog?

YOU DON'T HAVE TO DOMINATE to be effective; most dogs do much better with cheerful, confident leadership.

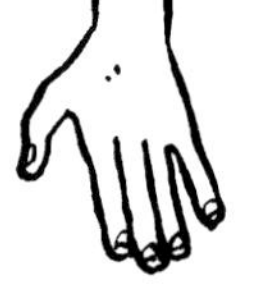

A In answer to the second part of your question, no, it isn't necessary to dominate your dog. But the extent to which your dog regards you as the leader in any situation isn't reflected by how gently or harshly she is trained. We all know people who can make themselves heard without raising their voices, and it's this sort of influence that you are looking to have with your pet. **Dogs who are kept as domestic pets live in a human world that runs on human rules, so it's only fair that they understand what those rules are—and your dog may need some help in seeing what your rules are from her viewpoint.** Your neighbor's views would have been more commonly held 20 or 30 years ago, when less interest was taken in how dogs' minds worked and in the canine perspective of how humans behaved.

There is no need to shout or push or pull a dog to train it effectively. Cross-species communication may call for more thought, but most dogs welcome leadership provided that they are taught your signals carefully, patiently, and consistently. A dog that is afraid of its human because it has been shouted at or pushed around in the course of its "training," may be just as obedient as a dog whose owner communicates calmly and cheerfully. What will be lost, though, in the fearful relationship is the enjoyment of happy, mutual cooperation between dog and human. And for most people, much of the pleasure of owning a dog comes from this joint understanding.

Ignore your neighbor and follow your own knowledge and instinct when training; both you and your dog will be the happier for it.

Index

Acknowledgments

With thanks to everyone at the Ivy Press for all their work in this book, and to Shawn Messonnier for casting his expert eye over the text.

For readers who would like to dig deeper into canine (and human) behavior, the books of Patricia McConnell (*The Other End of the Leash*, Ballantine Books, 2002, and *For the Love of a Dog*, Ballantine Books, 2007) and Suzanne Clothier (*Bones Would Fall from the Sky*, Grand Central Publishing, 2002) are invaluable guides, and inspired me to look at both the people and the dogs around me in a fresh light.